Guarneri

Also by Leonard Wibberley

Encounter Near Venus

Attar of the Ice Valley

Journey to Untor

Flint's Island

Beyond Hawaii

South Swell

Guarneri

Violin-maker of Genius

LEONARD WIBBERLEY

MACDONALD AND JANE'S · LONDON

Copyright © 1974 by Leonard Wibberley
First published in the United States of America
in 1974 by Farrar, Straus and Giroux, New York
Published in Great Britain in 1976 by
Macdonald and Jane's Publishers Ltd
Paulton House, 8 Shepherdess Walk
London N1 7LW

ISBN 0 356 08377 2

Printed and bound in Great Britain by
Redwood Burn Ltd.
Trowbridge and Esher

DEDICATED

with all its faults, to Mario Antonio Frosali,
Master Violinmaker of Legnano and Los Angeles,
and my own patient teacher in that great Art

Foreword

There is not enough material available to write an authentic biography of Guarneri del Gesù. Extensive research, undertaken largely by the Hill brothers of London (the great experts on violins), has produced little more than the dates of his birth, marriage, and death, and the fact that he had no children and, seemingly, no apprentices or helpers. There are persistent rumours that at one time he was imprisoned on a grave charge, but these have never been substantiated.

What follows, then, is very largely fiction, based on known facts, and rumours. I have done my best, however, in this fictional account, not to introduce incidents or elements utterly contrary to the character of Guarneri del Gesù as we know it. Some understanding of his character can be obtained from the study of his violins—the boldness of his work and his impatience with details, for example, perhaps indicate a bold and impatient man. Again, his father was not buried in the same grave as his mother as was then the practice. Indeed, she specified that he was not to be interred with her. This, and the fact that, as far as is known, the father made no violins for many years preceding his death, indicates some grave scandal, and John the half-wit is a wholly imaginary figure conjured up to explain these circumstances. Yet I do not think it an outrageous explanation of the darkness that seems to cling around Guarneri del Gesù and his father in his later years.

Perhaps the best way to look at this book is as a historical novel, containing, as such works must, some facts and a great deal of fiction—which might be fact or near to fact. I do not know that Guarneri del Gesù suffered a stroke at the end of his life. He did die young and the scrolls he carved in his last years strongly suggest some handicap.

Leonard Wibberley

*Hermosa Beach,
California*

Guarneri

Story of a Genius

1

It is common knowledge that there is no better country in the world than Italy, no better province of that country than Lombardy, and no better city than Cremona. You will certainly agree then that I was very fortunate to be born in Cremona in the year 1717, when the city was clear of that plague which had swept Holland and England many years before and still erupts here and there about the world. That it should have afflicted Italy at all was a matter of surprise to us, for Brother Cleophas said again and again that the plague wherever it broke out was the visitation of God on heretics who had thrown aside the teachings of Mother Church. Why then did it affect us, we asked.

"As a warning," said Brother Cleophas. "When I give you a box on the ears, it is not necessarily for something you have done, but for something that you may be thinking of doing." Sometimes he was wrong in giving such a blow, but in most cases I have to admit that he was right, and I tremble to think of what wickedness the whole of

Italy might have been guilty but for the warning of the plague.

Though being then very lucky in the place and time of my birth, I was not so fortunate in the matter of my parents. My mother died soon after I was born, and my father when I was a little over four years of age. He had been a charcoal burner, a trade essential to the whole of industry and one which should be honoured throughout the world. A moment's reflection will convince you that the charcoal burner, supplying small coals for smelting, for baking, for forging, for boiling—indeed, for every process requiring a high degree of heat—is the very seed of production. If then I am proud of my father's profession, you will have to agree that my pride was not without reason, seeing how much of the world's weight rests on the charcoal burner.

At my father's death, no one would have me. He had a brother in Rome and another in Venice and a sister married to a glazier and a member of the Glaziers Guild in Mantua. The rest of his family (there had been thirteen in all) had died of plague. None of the survivors could find room for me, and it was agreed that I would be put with the Benedictine brothers at their orphanage outside Cremona, where I could be fed and schooled for nothing, and taught some kind of trade.

Now, here is a curious thing that resulted from this upbringing. Most people, when they go into a monastery or a cathedral or any great building, find themselves awed and uncomfortable. But, brought up in such surroundings, what is more natural than that I should find myself completely at home among them, and come to love vast halls and corridors, lofty rooms, bright clerestories and solemn aisles. Now I am an old man and when I want to be happy (for old men are quite unhappy sometimes) I go to such a place and am soon soothed like a child who, out too long in the wind and the rain, has come home.

The orphanage to which I was taken at the age of four was that of the Holy Innocents and there were many who had been there since infancy. When a mother could not keep a baby (for whatever reason), she left it on the doorstep and rang the bell. The rule was that a minute must be allowed from the time the bell was rung before the door was opened, so that the mother might get away and so conceal her identity. In wintry weather that rule was not always followed, for many babies were left who were scarcely more than a day or two old—some by grandmothers, the mother having died in childbirth.

Now when I came to be taken to the orphanage and was left before the door, with a note pinned to me asking that I be taken in, Abbot Linus gave me the Christian name of Thomas, that day being the feast of St. Thomas. He gave me the family name of Soli (one alone), to signify that there was no one who would care for me. So Thomas Soli I became, born again, as it were, as Holy Scripture says we must all be to be saved.

Few boys stayed at the monastery after the age of twelve or thirteen, though the same was not true of girls, who were housed at the nearby convent of St. Cecilia.

Boys can be sent out to work as apprentices or sweepers, or messengers, or in some other needed capacity, when they are twelve or thirteen. Girls, however, are quite useless until they get married, and few will marry a girl who has not got some kind of dowry. So the girls had to stay on at the convent until they were young women, earning what little they could with needlework, selling bits of embroidery, doing a little cooking, or caring for rich children, until they had got together a dowry to make them more attractive to would-be husbands.

Of course, a beautiful girl had not much trouble in finding suitors. But it is only fair that a man, having to make do with a plain bride, should have a dowry of some sort as compensation. The uglier the girl, the harder she had to scrimp for her dowry.

We orphan boys were kept strictly separated from these orphan or unwanted girls. Indeed, we came to despise them, and they no doubt despised us. We were dressed as little monks, with our heads shaven, and they as little nuns, with their hair hidden. When we were brought into their presence, we felt ashamed and awkward. They felt the same. Among the boys, I was one of the bold ones. After all, the son of a charcoal burner is not going to be a mouse in the world. So I would contrive, on the great feast days when we were brought together with the girls to sing in church, to jostle the music out of the hands of one of them, or give her gown a tug, or stare at one until she blushed or had to lower her head.

This brought me many a thump on the head from

Brother Cleophas, who had bony knuckles and could fetch me a good blow without ever taking his eyes off the altar. But it gave me some prestige among the other boys.

When I got older, I began to notice that some of the girls were pretty, particularly a little one who I judge was about my age and with whom I once had to sing the Kyrie at Easter as a duo. For this we were dressed in the height of fashion—she in a panniered gown of brocade and with a silver wig on her head rising upward in clouds of curls to a tiny crown, and me in a suit of black velvet (for which Lombardy is famous) and white silk stockings, sparkling buckles on my shoes, and a small court sword at my waist. We walked, she on my arm, the whole length of the great church, coming to the altar rails among a storm of whispers. Brother Ambrose, who directed the choir, sounded the high D on his little pitch pipe.

"Kyrie eleison," she sang, her tiny voice as sweet as a bird in that vast building, and reaching to the G four tones above.

"Christe eleison," I replied, starting on that same high G, for a boy's voice, until it is broken, can reach that of any girl's. And so we sang the Kyrie together beautifully and then the great choir came thundering in with "Gloria in Excelsis Deo." It was all so beautiful it is a wonder that the whole church and everybody in it was not carried off gloriously on the moment to heaven.

During the Gloria we two walked back to take our places with the rest of the choir. Brother Ambrose, the choirmaster, was too busy with sopranos, altos, tenors, baritones, basses, and contrabasses, not to mention twenty string players, to pay any attention to us. We were strictly forbidden to speak to each other, and I had been solemnly enjoined at rehearsal not to allow the fact that I must give this little girl my arm to become an occasion of sin. In short, I must beware of the flesh, and at the orphanage I oftentimes trembled at the thought of those flames—a hundred miles high—that through all eternity consumed those who ignore that precept.

Still, it didn't seem to me that this pretty girl on my arm represented the flesh in the sense intended. So, coming back with her I sang, not the words of the Gloria, but: "What is your name? What is your name?"

She very quickly caught on and sang, "Annette. What is yours?" To when I replied in the middle of the great Amen: "It is Thomas Soli." By that time we had reached the choir loft and had to part with each other—a parting which caused me a surprising anguish.

That was the last I saw of that little girl Annette until Corpus Christi. I hoped that at that great feast we would again be chosen to sing a duo, but we were not. I caught only a glimpse of her among the crowd of other girls and I do not know whether she saw me.

At Christmas she was not in the choir, so I thought she might be ill. I could not of course inquire for her. I hurled prayer after prayer at heaven for her recovery, and especially besieged St. Thomas with my petitions. He is a good saint—none better. I will defend him before the whole of heaven, and on this and other occasions he showed his power.

At Candlemas I was standing at my appointed place in the choir, still without news of my duo partner, and I happened to glance at the place on the panelling where some time before I had indented my name with the corner of the crucifix on my rosary.

There was my name, "Thomas," and newly scratched below it was the name "Annette." So my prayers had been answered. She was well and cared for me. What more could I ask for of good St. Thomas in the whole world?

2

That year, being at the time twelve years of age, I met the first of many disasters of my life. I was the best singer among the boys. My voice was clear and steady and sure, and my ear was so good that I once ventured to tell Brother Ambrose that his pitch pipe was out of tune. And out of tune it proved to be.

Well, during Advent we were practicing for the Midnight Mass of Christmas, at which a cardinal from Rome was to be present. Brother Ambrose had written part of the music himself, with a four-part harmony for the Sanctus. All went well, until one rehearsal when, as I reached for a high F-sharp, my voice utterly disappeared. Worse than that, it returned in a second with a squeak like a dry hinge—a sound so terrible that the whole choir turned to glare at me.

Brother Ambrose pointed to me and put his fingers to his lips—that awful signal that quiets a boy guilty of the heavy sin of singing out of tune. I was appalled and angry. That terrible note, I knew, was entirely an accident. I could clearly hear in my mind the exact pitch required, and so, ignoring the discipline required of a member of a choir, I opened my mouth and tried again.

This time what came out was worse. Not even a goat could produce such a bleat. The choir stopped. Brother Ambrose turned on me fiercely. "Silence," he said. "Silence, Soli." And so, for the rest of the rehearsal, I stood there holding the music for others, mute and cast out.

Of course I knew that there was such a thing as a boy's voice breaking. I had heard this happen to many others. But not everybody's voice broke. Some found certain high notes gradually beyond their reach, while lower notes previously unsingable became available to them. They then moved over to sing with the contraltos or even the altos. But I now had no control over my voice at all. After the rehearsal, Brother Ambrose asked me to sing Guido's scale and I couldn't even get the "ut" in tune. I was told to avoid speaking unnecessarily and to eat garlic. I ate so many buds of garlic that other boys began to avoid me. It was no use. My voice remained unpredictable and uncontrollable and horrible.

In this disaster, Brother Cleophas was my comforter. He was in charge of boys' discipline, as Brother Ambrose was in charge of singing, and also taught mathematics. I was sent for and went to his study, wondering what I had done wrong, for a boy only visited Brother Cleophas's study when he had to be punished. But he was very kind to me. He gave me a pear and said I could eat it then and there if I wished, and that was kind, for otherwise I would have had to share it with everybody. Also he did not reprimand me when I surreptitiously wiped the juice off my mouth with the sleeve of my robe, for I had lost my handkerchief. He seemed, for once, to understand the many troubles which, however they try, afflict boys.

"Thomas," he said, "your voice will return to you in a while. But not the same voice. Probably tenor—perhaps baritone. However, the fact that it has gone temporarily is certainly a sign that you too should be going. You have been nine years here with us. It is time for you to go out into the world."

Everybody in the orphanage of course knew that the time would come when he would have to leave. I had given a lot of thought to what I would do at that time and I had the answer for it.

"Brother Cleophas," I replied, "I don't want to go out into the world. I believe I have had a very strong call from God and I ought to become a monk. Last night I had a dream . . ."

I told him about my dream. It was a good one, even though I was lying and had made it all up beforehand. But Brother Cleophas, it seemed, had dealt with too many boys who were being sent out into the world and did not want to go. In short, he did not believe me.

"If your dream was true and sent to you by God," he said quietly, "nothing will ever stop you joining the Benedictines or some other order later. But you must go out into the world first. Those who serve God give up the world for Him, Thomas. You can't give up something you know nothing about. The monastery is not a refuge from the world. It must be filled with men—not fugitives."

It was no use arguing. Out of the nest I had to go—out of those lovely silent corridors and great halls, out of the protection of those strong pillars in the church that I had come to look upon almost as people—out of the choir loft where my name was carved in the panelling with that of Annette below it.

That was what caused me the most pain. While Brother Cleophas talked about arrangements he had made for me to be apprenticed to someone in Cremona, I wondered whether he would understand that the real reason I couldn't go into the world was that I couldn't leave Annette—whose last name I did not even know.

I decided to be bold. After all, I was the son of a charcoal burner, and if I loved Annette, then I should prove this by speaking up.

"Brother Cleophas," I said, my voice hopping horribly all over the place, "I cannot leave Annette."

He stopped and said quietly, without the slightest trace of anger, "Annette? With whom you sang the Kyrie?"

"Yes, Brother Cleophas."

"Thomas," he said. "That Kyrie has been sung in duo by many boys and girls before your time. And each boy has thought that he could not leave the Annette with whom he sang it. But, like them, in a year or two you will have forgotten her."

"I will never forget her," I said with passion.

" 'Never' is a word that no human being can use," said Brother Cleophas. "Now forget Annette and I will take you into Cremona to meet your new master tomorrow."

On the following day, then, I put off my monk's robe and dressed in a suit of grey wool, which was second-hand, and the coat so big that my hands were drowned in the sleeves. I put aside my sandals and put on a pair of heavy shoes with hobnails in the bottom of them which slipped on the icy road. I was given another suit in a bundle with a spare shirt and a pair of stockings, and while I was dressing in the dormitory, some of the boys came in to say goodbye. They admired my clothes and were kind enough to ignore the fact that the sleeves were too long and that my hat was too small. They said I looked very well. They said they wouldn't forget me and asked me not to forget them. I told Carlo he could have my blanket, which was warmer than his, and I gave Mario a big piece of red sealing wax (it was as big as an apple) which I had stolen from Abbot Linus's office. And I exchanged rosaries with Fernando and gave a pencil box made of the best maple to Michele, who had lost his and been given one day in which to replace it.

They gave me a few things too. We promised that we would never forget each other wherever we went in the world, and then Brother Cleophas came for me, and feeling as though I were being taken to my execution, I left the monastery and got into a light farm cart to be driven down to Cremona.

I hoped that, whoever my new master would be, he

would at least live near the monastery, but we went right into the very heart of the city, which got noisier and noisier. Several times the cart had to stop because the traffic was so heavy, and though I pulled my tight hat as far down about my head as I could, boys passing by still noticed how short my hair was cropped as compared with theirs, which was shoulder length.

"Baldie" was the least of the names they hurled at me, and of course they did not fail to notice how long my coat was. With my voice in tatters, I couldn't hurl a word in return and so suffered every kind of indignity, until between sadness at parting with the orphanage and my friends and shame at the insults thrown at me, I was almost in tears. However, we Lombardians have certain signs we can make with our fingers to tell people what we think of them, and though the use of these signs is a grievous sin, I resorted to them at last and so evened matters up a little, though at the expense of my soul. I was very glad, however, when at last Brother Cleophas stopped the cart before a house on the corner of two streets, opposite a large cathedral.

"Here we are," he said, and pointing to the church, he added, "You can confess yourself over there for your behaviour while coming here." So my finger signs had not been lost on him, and indeed it is entirely true that Benedictines are enabled by special graces of God to see everything that goes on.

We got down from the cart and I looked at the flat, weatherworn front of the house which we were to enter.

There was a handwritten sign on a piece of board nailed up over the front door. The board was roughly cut in the shape of a viola da gamba, and the sign read:

> GIUSEPPE BATTISTA GUARNERI
> LUTHIER

3

The front door of Signor Guarneri's house was on the level of the street, or rather the square, in which the church, that of St. Dominic, was situated. It was a large door, solidly built to repel thieves, with a bellpull to one side, on which Brother Cleophas gave several hard tugs, so that the bell clanged vigorously.

When the sound had died away and no one had answered, Brother Cleophas jangled the bell again with even more vigour and this time was rewarded by an angry shout and a demand that we wait a moment. So we waited and after several minutes the door was opened and a tall, big-boned man, whose hair, uncombed, had been hacked off level with his neck, stood before us in no good temper.

"Do you think I am deaf?" he demanded. "Do you think the whole world can stop its work every time someone rings a door bell?"

"Good morning, Signor Guarneri," said Brother Cleophas, not the slightest disturbed by this reception. "I see you are in your usual good health."

"Oh," said the big man. "It's you. I have nothing to give. Nothing at all. Try two doors down. They are very wealthy there."

"It is I who have come to give to you," said Brother Cleophas. "Have you forgotten that you asked for a handy boy to help in your shop? Well, I have brought you the very best we have. A fine boy. He will be like a son to you. Yes. A son. And you like a father to him. Here he is."

I had been standing a little to the side, as is proper when one's elders are conversing. Brother Cleophas now motioned to me to come forward, which I did hesitantly. The man looked at me with only the most passing interest. Then he turned to Brother Cleophas.

"You have come at a very bad time," he said. "The glue will get cold. If it gets cold, I will have to do the whole work again. Goodbye." Without another word he disappeared into the house and my spirits rose immediately, for it seemed that the man did not want me and I could return to the orphanage.

But Brother Cleophas was not the man to bow to such a snub. He followed into the house, pulling me by the sleeve behind him, and we went down a dark corridor to a room on the right—a small room with a window opening on a courtyard, and a brazier of charcoal glowing in the middle. It was nice and warm in here, though a little stuffy.

The room looked like a neglected storehouse. There were stringed instruments of all kinds and in every condition strewn around. Some were suspended from the rafters by strings hooked onto nails, looking like so many plucked geese offered for sale in the market. Some leaned weakly against the wall, like tattered old men too exhausted to stand. Some were laid on their sides. Some had the tops off. Others lacked necks or scrolls. All, except one or two which seemed new, were to my eyes wrecked. I could not understand what was the use of keeping such a collection of junk, which I felt should be swept up or used for tinder. When I say instruments I do not mean just violins. There were violas da gamba, violas da braccio, violas d'amore, big violoncellos and bourdons, as well as lutes and guitars and cithers and even a harp or two—all of these in such profusion that you could scarcely move about that small room without finding some instrument in your way.

In the centre of the room was a bench and on it a tenor viol on which Signor Guarneri had been working when he was interrupted. The task was to restore the top, which had been removed so some repair could be made. The top was being put in place when Brother Cleophas rang the door bell.

"See," said Signor Guarneri, dipping a knife in some hot water and touching the glue on the instrument with it. "The glue is cold already. I have to take it off. The devil with door bells." He undid several clamps, removed the top of the gamba, and started to remove the glue with a cloth dipped in hot water.

When he had done this, so that there was not a particle of glue anywhere on the instrument, he put the viol down.

"No sense starting, if I am going to be interrupted," he said. "Let me tell you, Brother Cleophas, that to interrupt me when I am gluing an instrument is as bad a matter as to interrupt you when you are saying your office."

"You see then how badly you need this boy," said Brother Cleophas smoothly. "He will be able to answer the door bell for you and you will not be interrupted in your work."

Signor Guarneri now gave me another look, and I, in my turn, examined him, though surreptitiously. His clothes were almost those of a beggar's. His woolen stockings had holes and one slopped down his leg for lack of a garter. His shirt was soiled, and his breeches, which I think had been brown at one time, were now the colour of cobwebs. He wore an apron of the material called baize, covering him from neck to knees, but it was ragged at the edges and had several dark stains on it. His forehead was broad and powerful and his cheekbones pronounced. He was very handsome and powerfully built. But he had a look of anger about him, as if nothing in the world had ever pleased him. From the frown he turned on me, it was plain I was no exception to this rule.

"What is your name?" he asked.

"Thomas Soli, signor," I replied.

He pointed to one of the instruments in his shop. "What is that?" he asked.

"A lute, signor," I replied.

"And that?"

"A viola d'amore."

"And that?"

"I don't know, signor. I have not seen such an instrument before."

"What do you think it is?"

"Is it a mandolin?"

"No. It is a guitar in the English style." My replies gave him some slight satisfaction. For myself, I wondered at his questions. I had seen many of these instruments at the orphanage time and again, though I could not play them. A singer, after all, has his own musical instrument. He does not require another.

"He is a very good boy," said Brother Cleophas. "He has an excellent ear, and is quick to learn. You will certainly find him the greatest help. If there are difficulties, you have only to call us. Goodbye, signor. No doubt you are anxious to get back to your work."

He bowed to Signor Guarneri, and before another word could be spoken, he had left the little shop and was going down the corridor toward the street. With a sinking heart I heard the front door shut with a thump and a slight jangling of the bell and I was alone with my new master.

"Put your bundle over there," said Signor Guarneri. "And try not to annoy me. What I have to do would test the patience of a saint. If the door bell rings again, answer it and say that I have left for Rome and will not be back for four weeks. Or that I have the plague. Even that I have died."

"Yes, signor."

He looked at me and sighed. "Why couldn't they have

taken you to a cloth merchant?" he said. "With a cloth merchant you might have become rich. Poor fellow. As a luthier you must spend your life hungry."

He turned now to the tenor viol which he had been repairing. There was a pot of glue in an old iron saucepan, itself sitting on the brazier. He dipped a knife in the glue and, waiting for it to cool for a moment, put a little on his forefinger. Then he touched forefinger and thumb together. "Watch," he said. "After three or four times you must feel the skin start to stick. Otherwise the glue is too weak. If it is too weak, you have the job to do again. If it is too strong, the next man who has to work on the instrument will curse you for a bungler."

The glue seemed to satisfy him. He took a brush, nothing more than a set of bristles tied on the end of a stick, and putting it first in the hot water—to clean it, I suppose—shook it out, then put it in the glue. He applied glue to the top block of the viol and around the ribs and put the top on the instrument, working carefully to see the fit was perfect.

"A clamp," he shouted. It took little intelligence to know what he meant. There were thirty clamps at his feet. I gave him one. "Put it on," he said, still holding the instrument together. I did so. "Tighten it," he said. "Think of an egg. Too tight and you crush it. Too loose and it falls." So I tightened the clamp and he said immediately, "Another." Another was put on and then two more, all the time with a mounting sense of anxiety, until at last the glued top had been clamped back on the instrument. He looked carefully at the clamps, tightening one here and there, dipped his beggarly brush in the hot water, wiped off the excess glue which the pressure of the clamps had squeezed out. Only then did he relax.

"It is terrible in winter," he said. "Such repairs should only be done in the summertime. In the summertime, you have the sun to help you. That brazier there. What is it compared to the sun? It is nothing."

He held the viol to the brazier, turning it about so that a gentle heat could flow equally over the glue line. He continued meanwhile to examine the work and at last, satisfied, found a place to hang the instrument, still festooned with clamps, from the rafters.

That was my introduction to Signor Giuseppe Guarneri, who I learned later had the reputation of being easily the worst violinmaker in Cremona. The best of the violinmakers, a wealthy one, deferred to by everyone, was an old man who lived two doors down on the same street, his house and workshop also facing the Church of St. Dominic. His name was Antonio Stradivari and he was in his eighties at the time. He was a small man, a little stooped, with keen dark eyes and a nose like a hawk's beak. In contrast with my master, he was very neat and methodical in what he did. I was in his workshop many times and was always impressed by the tidiness. There were as many instruments there as in Signor Guarneri's, but they were hung in orderly rows. The whole place was cleaner and the light was better.

This is not to be wondered at. Signor Stradivari had two

sons, grown men, to help him, and several apprentices. Furthermore, he made violins for dukes and counts and cardinals and even kings. Doubt it if you wish. He made violins for the King of England and also for the King of France and the King of Poland, to name but three. My master had only me to help him. He did not really want even me.

As for trained workmen, he could not afford to pay them, and they would not work for him. If you wanted to say that a violin was poorly made, it sufficed to say that it was made by Guarneri. What workman would hire out to a man with such a reputation? Only the poorest.

Well, a boy cannot choose where he is to work. It was my lot on leaving the orphanage to work for the worst violinmaker in Cremona, and I had to make the best of it.

4

Signor Guarneri was married, and his household was run by his wife, Signora Cattarina, who had to help her a young girl of about my age, and also a half-witted man called John, who did the heavy work in the kitchen. I was afraid of this John. He talked to himself constantly and I would catch him at times watching me out of the corner of his eyes and mumbling something to himself in a way that frightened me. He was very strong and easily carried out the huge cans of ashes from the kitchen fire to be taken away by the carters and thrown in the dump outside the city walls or into the river, or on any vacant land available.

Most vacant land in Cremona became ash piles—the ashes were often mixed in with rubbish. In the summer the smell was very unpleasant and there were many flies. At nighttime you could see many rats darting here and there about the streets, sometimes in flocks. It was only natural that there should be a great many dogs in Cremona to keep the rats from taking over the city. Some of these dogs had owners, but many were wild, born in alleys or cellars, and learning to scavenge for themselves. At times there were dog fights, which were very exciting to watch, when a group of dogs, with all the daring of the Borgias, decided to invade the street or square which belonged to another group. It was splendid to watch the bristling manes, the bared teeth, the sudden dashes, and the slashing fangs and hear the growls and barks and yipes of these combats.

We apprentices knew the dogs of our area and of course cheered them in their encounters with strange dog packs, who also had their apprentice supporters. Sometimes the apprentices themselves came to blows, supporting their dogs, but that was only natural. I will confess that before a fight started I was often fearful, but when the first blow had been given, I enjoyed myself.

To finish with the condition of the streets of Cremona—in summer they were full of flies and rubbish and dust and smells. In winter they were at their best, for everything was frozen and the air delightful to breathe, even though the rubbish still was thrown out to moulder. In spring and in autumn, at both of which times we got rain, the streets became muddy, and if the rain was not heavy, the rubbish festered. But a heavy rainfall would wash the streets almost clean, everything flowing into a stream which threaded its way through the city, and then the cobbles glistened and the air, refreshed also by the rain, made everybody feel cheerful and young.

Signor Guarneri's house being opposite a church, the

streets were cleaner here than in other parts of the town. The steps of the church were a favourite place for beggars hoping for alms from people going in to Mass or to say a prayer. Begging was a great activity in Cremona, which itself attested to the wealth of the city. Who, after all, will beg in a poor town? You can readily gain some measure of the wealth of a city by the number of beggars in the streets.

But to return to Signor Guarneri's household: I was given a place to sleep on the fourth floor, where I had a great number of pigeons for company. These nested under the eaves of the roof, and kept up a constant flapping and muttering. This fourth floor was really an attic. The roof did not quite meet the walls, so that the place was well ventilated, and it was in the gaps between the roof and the wall that the pigeons nested. I had a bed, and a box in which to keep my clothes, and I was quite happy, though at times a little lonely. The rest of the place was taken up with lumber and boxes containing an untold quantity of bits and pieces of stringed instruments—pegs, bridges, fingerboards, tailpieces, and so on—together with an overflow of old instruments from Signor Guarneri's studio. The lumber used to make or repair instruments was kept here to season.

The third floor was empty and Signor Guarneri and his wife and the young girl Celeste lived on the second floor. John, the half-wit, lived in the kitchen and had the best quarters of all, for there he was sure to be warm even on the coldest nights. My master, taking pity on me in the cold attic, said I could sleep in the kitchen with John, but since I did not trust him, I remained where I was.

My duties were very simple. For a while I did nothing but answer the door bell and run little errands. Cremona is famous for many things, foremost among them her churches. Everybody has heard of the famous cathedral built hundreds of years before, which has beside it the great Torrazzo, the tallest tower in the whole of Italy. Then there is the Church of St. Agatha, and St. Michael, and St. Sigismondo, in which there are many beautiful paintings. These all had their choirs and their musicians, and there were in addition many wealthy merchants in the city who had private bands of musicians. Besides the silk and cloth and dyeing trades, Cremona was famous for her musicians, the greater number of whom played stringed instruments. So there was a constant stream of them coming to my master's house to have their instruments repaired or adjusted—to have new strings put on or new bridges fitted, or pegs eased. They all wanted such repairs done at once. They all wanted to see Signor Guarneri personally and most of them wanted to stand there and watch while he worked.

I have told you that Signor Stradivari, a very wealthy man and easily the most famous violinmaker in Cremona, lived but two doors down the street from us. Well, there were two other violinmakers on the same square, Signor Carlo Bergonzi, who occupied the premises between ours and those of Signor Stradivari, and Signor Girolamo Amati, who lived on the south side of the square. If that was not enough, up the street from us, opposite the Dominican Monastery, which was attached to the Church of St. Dominic, lived yet another maker, Signor Vincenzo Ruggieri, so that there were five violinmakers within a few hundred yards of each other.

That was plenty for musicians from Cremona (and other cities as well) to choose from. Those who wanted new instruments went to Stradivari or Bergonzi or Ruggieri. It was only if they had very little money that they came to my master. The same was true of repair work. If they could afford to spend a good deal on repairs, they went to one of the other violinmakers. If they hadn't much money or wanted to drive a hard bargain, they came to Signor Guarneri.

Why such an unequal state of affairs? It puzzled me for a long time, but there was no one cause to which to point. First, my master had no family other than his wife to help him and take his part. He had an older brother, Peter. But he lived in Venice, where he had a good reputation as a maker, repairer, and player. He never came to Cremona to see his younger brother. Signor Guarneri's father, Joseph, was alive and living in Cremona. But some terrible scandal attached to his name. He had given up the business of making and repairing instruments and lived obscurely, almost secretly, in another part of the city. My master had to support him out of his earnings and, for the sake of his own reputation, forbade his father to come to see him. So you see there was a feeling of distaste for my master about the city because of the unspoken scandal concerning his father, which certainly did not encourage business.

In short, with so much competition from others, and a tainted name, Signor Guarneri had to take what work he could get. He got the work others refused. He was paid only in trifles and then irregularly. My master worked hard and well on his repairs, but because he got paid only a coin or two, his work was little valued. Bergonzi or Stradivari could demand several ducats for a repair for which my master received only a soldo or two.

When it came to making instruments, he could not afford to lavish the care on them that Stradivari did, for instance. He would get only a small sum for a new violin and so had to turn them out quickly and somewhat roughly. In short, poor pay brings rough work, and rough work brings poor pay.

I am sure that if the King of France had thought to ask my master to make him an instrument, he could have made one just as beautiful as those of Signor Stradivari two doors down. But it was not the King of France but a tavern player who came to him for a new violin. Does one make beautiful instruments to be played in taverns and on street corners and at fairs—to be wet with wine and thrown about, snatched from hand to hand, and bumped and dropped and scratched? Of course not.

My master, then, made rough-looking instruments. He was called the worst violinmaker in Cremona, as I have told you. I was called the assistant of the worst violinmaker in Cremona. One of the helpers of Stradivari called me that to my face one day. "My master's varnish," he said, "which I help to make, is acknowledged the most beautiful in the city. Yours is hardly fit for putting on picture frames."

"Well," I said, "my master is working on a new varnish with more red in it. And here is the secret ingredient." And I punched him on the nose, making it bleed. I was of course soundly whipped by Signor Guarneri for this outburst but gained a little respect among my fellow apprentices nonetheless.

One thing more I have to point to as the cause of my master's poor pay and rough work. I will put it plainly. He was often drunk. He hid this very well from me for a week or two after I came to him. At times I thought his speech a little thick and low, his hand slow and eye uncertain. But I was only a boy and knew little of drunkenness and assumed that he was not well. His wife told me the truth.

"Soon he will spend everything I have managed to save," she said. "Then he will pawn his tools. Then he will pawn his instruments. Then he will pawn instruments that do not even belong to him. Then he will send me to borrow money from Signor Stradivari to get his tools back. It is shameful. But it cannot be helped."

So it turned out. When I had been with him only two months, my master one day started drinking heavily and by the end of the week he had spent every coin in the house, and pawned all the tools that weren't hidden from him. He pleaded for money for wine, then he threatened, and then, when he had taken everything he could get, he disappeared. It was my job to find him.

I hunted for him in all the taverns, starting at the more

expensive and going lower and lower until I was in places where I felt it unsafe even to open the door. When this happened, John the half-wit became more and more distracted. He went continually from floor to floor and room to room of the house day and night, searching for Signor Guarneri. At last, after searching and inquiring for him in every wineshop in the city, I found my master stumbling along the banks of the river in freezing weather without a coat or a hat.

"Master," I cried, "what is the matter with you? You are sick."

"Sick?" he said, staring at me. "Sick? It is worse than that. I am alone. Always alone. Alone."

I thought him raving and, taking his arm, dragged him home. That was my first experience of these bouts. There were others. And it was always the same. At the end of them he could offer only the one explanation. "I am alone," he would cry. "Always, always alone."

Sometimes he wept bitterly when he had been fetched home. Sometimes he set his face like a man accepting some terrible punishment. It took him several days to recover from these fits of drinking, during which time he could do no work. I would tell his clients that he was sick. Some of them smiled a knowing smile, but few expressed any sympathy, for they knew what his sickness was.

I tried to encourage these clients to come back, or if they owed him money (which very many did), I begged them for some payment so I could get my master's tools. Some paid, but many found an excuse for not paying.

Gradually my master would recover. Gradually he would face the realities of what he had done—the tools gone, instruments pawned, some even which did not belong to him. Then, terribly silent, he would drag himself to Signor Bergonzi or Signor Stradivari to beg tools or a little money or even work to get started again. I have to say immediately that they always helped him—Signor Stradivari the first to do so.

Once, after such an episode, when I went to Stradivari's shop to beg the loan of a small gouge, the great man was himself there. Hearing my request (made of course to one of his assistants), he himself gave the gouge to me and, inquiring what work was in hand, gave me also two small planes with curved soles and told me to come directly to him for anything else that was needed.

"What is your name?" he asked.

"Thomas Soli, signor," I replied.

"Soli," he repeated. "It is a name well matched to your master. Do not disrespect him, Thomas. Work well for him. For all his faults, he is no ordinary man." He paused. "He may yet be remembered longer than any of us," he added.

5

That first time that my master was overtaken by one of his fits, when there was little money for food in the house, I consulted with Signora Cattarina and we decided that we must make every effort to sell some of the numerous viols, cithers, guitars, and lutes which crowded the shop. A number of these Signor Guarneri had had to take in trade, either as part payment on one of his violins or as part payment for work done on some other instrument. When there was a fair or a holiday, he occasionally sold some of these old instruments, for what is a holiday without a tune? In between times they just littered his shop.

Therefore, we agreed that they should be cleaned up and I would take them about, door to door, and see what could be done. I started out on a raw day in March, with a number of viols and lutes in a wheelbarrow, under an old cloak, which I took through the streets calling, "Viols for sale," and in fact making a little tune to the words.

Of course my voice had not yet returned, so it cracked time and again. But I had to compete with the other vendors of goods and services—the small-coals man, and the knife sharpener, the tinker, the glazier, and the chimney sweep, all of whom had a little song or cry to give advertising their wares.

I devised, then, a little tune around the dominant of the D-major scale to match their cries. I would write my little cry out for you but that is hardly necessary, for when I tell you that I ended it on a tierce of Picardy, you will understand immediately how appealing it was.

It brought many people to look at my wares, and one or two who thought I was buying secondhand instruments and wanted to know what I would offer for viols without fingerboards and lutes without pegs. These I first of all turned away. But that was not good business. The people of Lombardy are the world's greatest bargain hunters. They will buy anything if they think it is a bargain, whether they wish it or not.

So I soon learned to take the old broken lutes as part payment on the good ones I had. In matters of buying and selling, lies are of course permitted. Otherwise, how else could merchants survive? Some of the instruments offered me, though broken, were occasionally better than those I had for sale. On these I would give only a contemptuous glance and say they were good for nothing but kindling. Then I would put up the price of the instrument I had to sell, and when the bargain was concluded, I had got the full price of the instrument I sold, plus an old one on top.

You will never get better mandolins and lutes than those made in Venice. No. Not even in Cremona. I got several Venetian lutes in this way. When I returned home at the end of my first day of selling, Signora Cattarina shook her head in disappointment. "You haven't sold a single instrument," she said, seeing the mound on the wheelbarrow.

I enjoy surprising people. "I had to take these in trade," I replied.

"Dolt," she said. "Do you think we need more of those boxes? You are as bad as Signor Guarneri."

"I had to take these in trade," I replied quietly, "but if you think I ought to give them back, I will have to return the money too." Then I took out the piece of cloth in which I had the money wrapped. It came to three lire and twenty-four soldi. Signora Cattarina gave a squeal of delight when I showed her the coins, and Celeste, always in the shadow, looked at me as if I were a god.

"This is more than we make in a week," said Signora Cattarina.

"A mere trifle," I replied. Let others be modest. It is my opinion that one must stand up for oneself.

I was that night given a place closer to the kitchen fire and as much cabbage soup as I could hold, and I could hold a lot, for I had scarcely eaten all day.

Thereafter, once a week, I took a barrow of instruments around the streets of Cremona and could reckon to gain a lira or two for my work, though I must confess that there were weeks when I sold nothing. But I was not put down by these bad weeks, for as Brother Cleophas had often said, "God, who sends the sun, is also entitled to send the frost and the wind."

Now, as you see, I had more to do than answer the door bell. I began also to handle the selling of instruments and the business of collecting for repairs. This was very delicate work.

If they are to be believed, musicians never have any money, but are always expecting some. When it arrives, unfortunately, it is always needed for something other than paying the repair bills on their instruments. Signor Guarneri was never able to refuse to give a musician an instrument he had repaired even when the bill was not paid. He felt that the man needed it to earn his living. I devised a better plan.

When a customer could not pay his bill, I kept his instrument, but so that he would not be without the means of making a living, I loaned him one which was much worse. That system worked wonders. It was never more than a week before the customer was back, moaning about the poor instrument, at times very angry and threatening to wrap it around my neck. But he always ended by producing the money to pay for his own.

In a little while, using only firmness and the amount of sense an orphan has to develop to hold up his end with other boys, we had a comfortable income coming into the shop. Signora Cattarina, who had always been cold and snappish, warmed up. Signor Guarneri had fewer days when he would not say a word to anybody. Even Celeste, who besides being timid was also lumpish, looked a little happier. The only person who was not pleased was the half-wit John. His initial dislike for me grew worse. He was jealous of my place by the fire and such trifles as

Signora Cattarina giving me my soup before him. If Signor Guarneri showed me any favour, John would give me a fierce look and mumble away to himself in a fury. Once he put a shovelful of ashes in my bed, and another time, when I went out into the courtyard, he dropped a heavy barrel suddenly beside me, so that if I had not moved, he would have broken my foot.

I could not understand why he disliked me so much. It was no use speaking to him. He was incapable of talking, his muttering being only a series of noises which did not form words. He had not enough brains to learn to speak. That is the truth of the matter. Nothing I could do would please him. The only person who could get him to behave himself was Signor Guarneri. When he rebuked John for misbehaving, John would hang his head like a beaten cur and drag himself about the place in misery until forgiven. I tried never to be alone with him, for the truth is he frightened me.

After a while Signor Guarneri decided he would show me something about instrument making. Perhaps he had been talking to Brother Cleophas and had been told that I had a good ear. In any case, he wanted to get a lot of violins ready for the Whitsun festival. At the fair he always had a little booth with violins hung up on lines for sale. Signora Cattarina hated this fair, for my master was invariably drunk for a week after, so there was no profit from it, no matter how many instruments he sold.

In any case, one day in January he threw me a piece of spruce and said, "What do you think of that for a violin?"

I had watched him select wood, so I knew what to look for. The grain was not the best. It was broad and wavy. Also, there was a knot at the upper end of the piece that could not be cut up. "It is very poor," I said.

"Bah," he replied. "You are not going to make a violin for the King of Prussia. You are going to make one for a tinker. So never mind how it looks. How does it sound?"

I picked up the piece of wood, and hanging it between my thumb and middle finger before me, I tapped it with my knuckle as I had seen him do. To my surprise, the tone came out clear as a little bell—the tone itself firmly, and another tone a fifth above it, though less distinct. I tapped again, with the same surprising result.

"Well?"

"It sounds very good."

"Can you sing the tone?"

My voice failed me and I could not. Impatiently, he gave me one of his violins and told me to match the tone on its strings. It took me only a few tries to find it on the lowest, or G, string. He was pleased.

"That is the first secret of violinmaking," he said. "A good ear. Otherwise, you will never be anything but a cabinetmaker. When it comes to thinning and shaping the top and bottom plates of a violin, you must do this with your ear more than your eye. In Venice and Mantua they consult only their eye." He had, I found, a poor view of violinmakers of those two cities, perhaps because his brother, with whom he had some quarrel, had lived in both of them.

He first told me to make a mould for a violin. A mould is nothing more than a solid piece of wood in the shape of the body of a violin but with the corners taken out. This shape is the inside shape, and the corners are left out because they are part of the violin and not of the mold, which of course is only there to bend the ribs of the instrument around. I copied one of his moulds exactly and ruined three pieces of wood before I had one made I could show him.

"Why do you take so long?" he demanded.

"It is difficult to cut out the curves, signor," I replied. "The saw keeps running into the wood."

"Don't press on the saw," he said. "Let the teeth do the work. A saw is not a knife. You don't need force." I expected praise for my mould. It was certainly better than his. The two sides were equal, whereas those of his mould were lopsided. I pointed this out to him.

"You should work for Signor Bergonzi next door," he said.

"Why?" I asked.

"He likes a perfect shape. It is not a shape I am making. It is a sound. Whether it is lopsided or not doesn't matter to me. All I care is how it sounds."

He picked up a violin which he had finished only that week. It had no varnish on it, but had been strung up. He snatched up a bow and tuned the violin. I have seen players take five minutes to tune, but he tuned in a few seconds. Quickly he ran up the octaves on the G, D, A, and E strings. Then he played the G-major scale in thirds through two octaves, and then broke into a set of variations by Corelli on an old tune which is known to everybody. It is called "La Folia."

A glorious, full, vibrant sound poured from the instrument. It was a sound as warm as summer, full of life, rich as wine. This was the first time I had heard one of the violins of my master played. The volume of sound was like that of an organ, the tone especially beautiful on the lower strings. It filled the whole shop and flooded the street beyond. I listened openmouthed. Others entered the shop, customers I thought, but I took no notice of them. It was only when Signor Guarneri stopped and put down the violin that I turned and saw standing there Signor Stradivari and Signor Bergonzi.

Signor Stradivari, without a word, came forward and took the violin from my master. He took the bow, tuned the instrument, and started to play. Again the sounds, as warm as heart's blood, filled the studio. I could recognize that sound anywhere, though Signor Stradivari's style of playing was inferior to that of my master. When he had finished, he looked at the instrument closely, shook his head, and said, "Signor, the voice is that of an emperor, the clothing that of a beggar."

"Signor Stradivari," replied my master, a little annoyed. "As God is concerned only with the soul and not with the body or its appearance, so I am concerned only with how my instruments sound and not how they look."

"Nonetheless," said the other, "if you took more pains, you could sell your violins to kings."

"Signor," said my master, "I do better than that. As you will see from the label, I give my violins to Christ—the King of Kings." And this was so, for, in every instrument he made, my master put the letters "I.H.S.," signifying that they were dedicated to Jesus, the Saviour of Man.

6

The Whitsun fair in Cremona that year was commonly agreed to have been the best since the Austrian wars, when the French had possession of the city. I will give you now an anecdote concerning that time which I heard from Brother Cleophas. The French had a very bad general whom the Austrian army under Bellona captured in its attack on the city, though the attack itself failed. This produced a little jingle, composed by the French soldiers, which went:

Frenchmen: three cheers for Bellona,
Our fortune could hardly be grander,
We still have our hold on Cremona,
But have happily lost our commander.

The French are a very witty people and, all in all, their short occupation of Cremona was preferred to that of Austria. They certainly benefited the instrument makers of the town, for, next to the Italians, the French are the most musical people on earth. Alas, they cannot sing. A

Frenchman singing, it is generally agreed, brays like a donkey, for their language is so nasal. Being unable to sing, then, they are great purchasers of instruments, and during the French occupation the luthiers thrived and the fame of Cremona instruments, especially those made by Signor Stradivari, was spread. As a direct result of the French occupation, he received many commissions for violins, and cellos. Violas, which are the instrument between the violin and the cello, were not much in demand. In any case, they could readily be made by cutting down tenor violins—that is, large violins tuned an octave below the violin itself and played between the legs like a gamba, being too big to put under the chin.

From this it will be seen that wars, bad as they are, still produce some good results. Up to the time of the French occupation of Cremona, the violins of an Austrian maker, Jacob Stainer, had generally been preferred in Europe. After the war, the fame of the Cremona instruments spread. Furthermore, several French families of wealth and position settled in Cremona, where they found living cheaper than in France, and plenty of entertainment available. So that terrible war, followed as usual by an outbreak of plague, still had its benefits and, by the spread of good music from Italy, helped to civilize the French.

In the year of which I write, that is to say 1732, there was a feeling of prosperity in the air. There had been no war involving Lombardy for two decades. Trade was good. The silk business in particular flourished. There had been a great hatching of silkworms, free of disease, and we could look for a record production of fine cocoons, from which of course the silk is obtained. All these factors combined to produce a great Whitsun feast and fair. At the Church of St. Dominic, the monks decided to revive some old customs that year, in particular the dropping of balls of fire from the top of the church, behind the altar, to symbolize the tongues of flame which had descended on the Apostles on the first Pentecost, when they had received the Holy Ghost. This was of course done at the dawn Mass, and was a huge success. Many hundreds of children, clad in white robes, were brought for baptism and the singing was of the finest.

All the violinmakers and their assistants formed a string choir for the dawn service. They were placed to the side of the altar, though outside the rails (there was not room enough for them in the choir loft), and the effect was splendid. At the "Veni, Sancte Spiritus," introduced by the violins, I, though far in the back of the great church, could hear my master's instrument, bold and free, singing out that beautiful appeal. It did not overshadow the violin of Signor Stradivari. That is not my meaning. But it sang distinct in its own colour and I was compelled to thump a fellow apprentice who was standing beside me and whose whispering disturbed me. Such blows, if a proper view is taken of them, are certainly acts of grace, being given, after all, in the service of God.

After Mass, began the fair, which lasted for a week and brought us visitors from every part of Europe. The streets were decorated with flags, with buntings, and with wreaths and chains of flowers. Every statue wore a wreath, every window had hanging from it the brightest cloths in the possession of the household—many of them Turkish carpets of magnificent colours. The centre of the city, in which the fair was held, was blocked off from all but foot traffic. There were fireworks displays every evening, dancing, masques, processions, bear baitings, amazing displays by jugglers, particularly a troupe from Germany, in which three men handled as many as thirty clubs flying through the air without anyone dropping a single club. There were acrobatic displays, and tightrope walkers stretched their lines between the twin towers of the cathedral and walked across the gap like flies on a thread.

In all this confusion and excitement, I will not pretend that the booth of my master Signor Guarneri made any great splash. The City Fathers, of course, allotted the spaces for each booth, and a portion was set off for the makers of violins. It was here that we spread out our instruments, line on line of violins, hanging by their scrolls, made by Signor Guarneri, as well as many older instruments which he had taken in trade.

Signor Guarneri was a very fast workman. With me to help him, he could make a violin in a week. I did the rough work, the gouging out of the wood from the top and back plates, the rough shaping of the scrolls. He did the finished work. Some of the scrolls were not so handsome—certainly not as good as those of Signor Bergonzi, who had the booth next to us, or Signor Ruggieri, who was across the way.

Some of the instruments were "in the white"—that is to say, they were not varnished. Varnishing is the longest part of violinmaking, because of the time each coat takes to dry. The unvarnished instruments we sold cheaper, the buyer undertaking to do the varnishing himself. After all, the varnish is only there to protect the wood and make the instrument look pretty. There was no secret to this varnish as some pretend. It could be bought made up in any chemist shop or obtained from any sign painter or artist's studio.

Some people liked instruments with a golden varnish. Some liked a brown colour, and others still a golden red, or even a reddish colour. So if they bought an instrument unvarnished, they could please themselves about the colour.

Ours was the only booth at which an unvarnished instrument could be bought. However, these unvarnished instruments did not have Signor Guarneri's ticket inside with the initials which he had adopted: "I.H.S."—Jesus, Saviour of Mankind. He called them "fair violins," and they did not represent his best work.

I slept at the booth to guard our goods, and Signora Cattarina cooked our meals there to save money. We did very well. It was my job to call people's attention to our wares, which I did by singing my little song with the tierce of Picardy at the end, or by playing a jig on one of the violins.

47

Although I had had no training in playing an instrument (a singer, as I have said before, has in his voice his own instrument given him by God), I soon learned to play a few jigs on the violin. Furthermore, scrupulously trained by Brother Ambrose, I played them in tune, which is more than can be said for many others I heard scraping away. I did not play as well as Signor Guarneri. He was a master and was sometimes engaged to play performances in some great house. But I had a quick ear and did so well that a man who owned a dancing bear offered me a job as fiddler. All I had to do was fiddle while the bear danced (stopping only to pick up the coins thrown to us), and I could have one quarter of what was collected and all my meals. But, thinking the matter over, I decided to decline the offer. Although the dancing bear and its master made good money (he, lacking a fiddler, beat a drum for it), it seemed to me that fairs might be few and far between and there would be many hungry days in his service.

My master behaved himself very well during the fair. To be sure, he drank a little wine (it is well known that a man loses all his strength if he drinks nothing else but water). But he did not drink to excess. He got along well with his wife and bought her a very pretty bonnet and a pair of shoes at a neighbouring booth. He dropped the surly mood which he had shown almost since the day I joined his household. He was full of good spirits and altogether a different man. His black hair, which he now combed daily, glistened in the early summer sun, and his face, pale from the confinements of winter, was soon tanned a golden colour, which showed his even white teeth to perfection when he smiled. Truly I saw in those days of the fair that my master was two men—one tortured, sullen, haunted by loneliness which he could not explain, and the other cheerful, outgoing and the best of company. Signora Cattarina watched this change with reserve. She would smile now and again to be sure. Once, even, she laughed, but as the fair progressed, as we sold more instruments, as my master became more and more popular with his wit and his charm (particularly among the ladies, who were quite naturally attracted to him), Signora Cattarina became more and more thoughtful.

"Soon comes the storm," she said, putting me thoroughly out of sorts with her. Did she, after all, not believe in the grace of God? Did she seriously doubt that good could in the end overcome evil, that the better nature of my master could not, in the end, triumph over his darker side?

"Signora," I said, "why expect a storm? Surely it is possible for people to change, particularly if they offer up prayers to God?"

"What prayers?" she asked.

"Signora," I remonstrated. "Every violin your husband makes contains a prayer, for it is made in the name of Christ Himself."

"If only I could get him away from Italy to Austria, where people are more sensible," she said. She was from the Tyrol and although she had lived now several years in Cremona, she still thought the Tyrolese better than the people of Cremona.

We made a lot of money at the fair. We were able to

pay back what remained of the debt to Signor Stradivari. The pawned tools had already been redeemed, of course, and Signora Cattarina every day counted the amount taken in and, holding out only what was needed for current expenses, put the rest away in some secret place of her own. This at length annoyed my master. At first he thought it only prudent, for there were of course many cutpurses about, and the stocks and pillories in the public places of the town were never without customers.

After a while, however, my master began to resent the hiding away of the money, suspecting (which was true) that it was being hidden from him as much as from thieves.

One evening at the close of the fair he demanded a few lire, as he had favours to repay among the people of the town.

"Why not send them to me, signor?" said Signora Cattarina. "I will pay them to the last soldo. Or, if it is a gift of hospitality, perhaps they will come to our house when we can have a good dinner together as a mark of our esteem and gratitude."

"Heavens," said Signor Guarneri. "What are you making such a big to-do about? I am asking you for one or two lire. Is it too much to give me?"

He was given the money and we all held our breath, wondering whether this was but the beginning of another drinking bout. But he surprised us. He went to a tavern or two, had a few drinks with his friends, drank perhaps more than he should, but he returned in good humour and without making demands for further money. It seemed that he had managed to exorcise the sullen, self-torturing demon which had previously possessed him.

A great ball was to be given, at the conclusion of the fair, at the Château of St. Croix, at which the nobility and the more affluent merchants from Turin, Milan, and Venice would be present. Being so fine and sure a player, my master was asked to lead the orchestra of the Disuniti Academy on that occasion. The Disuniti (or disunited) was a group formed in mockery of a previous academy of Spanish, who became so touchy on points of honor (who was to sit in the first chair, the second chair, and so on) that they were finally disbanded. (That had been in the days of Spanish control of Cremona, before we were handed over to the Austrians after the War of the Spanish Succession, which was really not of the slightest concern to us in Cremona, though naturally we suffered from it.)

My master was pleased to accept this honor and, declining the kind offer of a Stradivari violin for the occasion, elected to play on one of his own. The greater number of the musicians played on cheap instruments anyway, some of them on instruments obtained from my master, and others on older instruments from Brescia.

I, of course, could not attend so great an occasion. Besides, I had no good clothes to wear. But everybody agreed that my master played splendidly, though there were some who thought he overpowered the other players.

Signora Cattarina was permitted to eat with the servants at the ball. In short, everything was a great success.

The storm she had looked for did not come, and in fact Signor Guarneri received several orders for instruments to be made of better-quality wood, for one of which he was to receive three lire—almost half the amount Signor Stradivari could command for his violins.

It certainly seemed to me then that we were on the road to fortune, and I thought happily that in a few years I would be established in a good trade and could claim Annette, who by that time could be expected to have collected a little dowry of her own.

7

Two years went by and, all in all, we prospered. My master, to be sure, had three or four of his bouts, but never got to the point of using all his money and selling all his tools. There was no explanation for these fits. Something gnawed within him, and when this was beyond bearing, off he would go to the taverns. That he did not on these occasions spend every soldo in the house, he had Signora Cattarina to thank for. She took any surplus of money there might be and invested it in the silk business.

Money for the raising of silkworms is always hard to come by for small operators, who have little or no banking credit. Mulberry leaves in large quantities have to be gathered constantly. The worms have to be kept clean in their racks. Any that seem sick must be immediately disposed of. In short, a great deal of labour is required before the beautiful cocoons are produced and sold to the manufacturers for reeling. All this takes money, and Signora Cattarina, saving a little here and there, was able to lend out modest sums at fifteen and twenty percent.

When he had been drinking, Signor Guarneri stormed and railed against this use of his money and complained that he had not enough to buy good wood for his violins. But it was for wine and not wood that he wanted the money at such times. It was true, however, that fine wood for violins was hard to find and costly to buy. Some blamed this on the recent wars, but the increase of trade and prosperity which after a while followed those wars was also a cause. Where people had been content in olden times with plain pine for furniture for their homes, they now, imitating the nobility, wanted something more attractive. Maple in particular was in demand for sideboards and dressers, and even billiard tables. What was left for violinmakers was high-priced, and my master could afford to buy only small pieces. Sometimes he had to join two or three pieces together to get enough to make a back for a violin. He never had a piece big enough to make a cello or a viola, and never receiving an order for one or the other, he never made such instruments. Many makers in Venice and Mantua made violins with backs of beech or poplar or pearwood, finding maple too expensive. Signor Guarneri would not use such wood.

"Why not?" I asked him one day while I was trying to shape some corner blocks for a violin under his direction—they are very difficult to fit.

"Let the furniture makers use beech and pearwood and poplar, and leave the maple to us," he growled.

With Signor Stradivari, matters were different. Receiving orders for the best instruments, he could afford the best materials. For instance, he used willow for the corner blocks and linings of his violins. We used what was left over from the spruce from the top for this purpose. In my journeys about the city selling old instruments, I kept an eye open for any wood I might find in the streets of use to us. In one house which was being pulled down I got several pieces of a banister which was of maple and with which Signor Guarneri was pleased. There was a coach-house behind the main square where there were several broken-down vehicles. On one of them I noticed a maple panel, which had been partially painted brown. I bought it for a few coins and my master was able to make two violin backs from it. Such finds, however, were windfalls and generally we were very short of good wood.

My voice had now returned to me. I sang as well as ever, though in the tenor register. I sang at the High Mass each Sunday in the Church of St. Dominic and sometimes at the Church of San Prospero, which was a little farther away and to which Signor Guarneri sometimes went. I could play the violin quite well now, and under Signor Guarneri's eye I had made two violins, both of which, alas, sounded poorly.

This was a great surprise to me. It was generally agreed that I was a good woodworker and had a good ear and followed instructions minutely. Indeed, at a glance, my violins looked better than those of my master. They were more neatly made. My purfling, which is the edging or hem of wood let into top and bottom plates to prevent them splitting, was much more elegant. My scrolls were also more exact. I was never in a hurry to finish an instrument, but took pleasure in getting everything right. When my violins were finished, however, they were a terrible disappointment. Under my ear, they sounded well enough. Twenty feet away, their voice was thin.

Naturally, I blamed the wood. For one of the instruments I had used part of that piece I had got from the coachhouse, a piece which had been painted. The paint I decided had ruined the properties of the wood. Unfortunately for this excuse, my master made a violin of the rest of the same piece and the tone was splendid. Well, then, I thought, there was merely some adjustment which had to be made and my violins would sing like blackbirds. The sound post was either bad or in the wrong place. Or I needed to cut a new bridge. But when I had attended to all these details of adjustment, the violins sounded just as poorly. There was no escaping the fact that, handsome as they looked, they were inferior.

"What is wrong with them?" I demanded.

Signor Guarneri shrugged. "It isn't one big thing that is wrong with them," he said. "It is a thousand little things."

I waited for him to tell me just one of these thousands of little things, but he went on with his work. When after two days he had not told me, I asked him just to mention one of them.

"Do you expect to make a good violin after only two years of teaching?" he asked. "I worked ten years with my father before I could be sure of making a good instrument. He worked the same time with his father. In fact, he spent all his life trying to make better instruments. He . . ." Then he broke off and said no more for a while. Eventually he added, "Maybe you will never make a great violin. We cannot all be Stradivari."

That was not the first bitter reference he made to the rich old maker, always generous to him, who lived but two doors away. Another's success, after all, is hard to bear in the face of your own failure. If Stradivari had only turned out one or two bad-looking instruments—if he had only now and again slipped and failed to produce something first class, my master would have found his triumphs easier to bear. But the fact is that Stradivari broke up any instruments that looked bad or sounded bad, and my master could not afford to do that.

It was not easy for him, I assure you, to see the flunkies of counts and of dukes, of bishops and cardinals and the wealthy bankers of Venice, calling on Signor Stradivari to pick up instruments ordered two or three years before, counting out the golden coins on his workbench, bringing him presents of beautiful pieces of cloth, or rings and snuffboxes from their masters, while he had only poor musicians for customers—most of them merely wanting an instrument repaired. At times I know my master blamed the success of Signor Stradivari for the ruin of his own father, who now no longer made any instruments and lived a sort of hidden life. He felt that Stradivari had overwhelmed his father, deprived him of the fruits of his life as a violinmaker. He felt that the same applied to himself. His constant excuse for not making better-looking instruments was the bitter, mocking question, "Who can compete with Stradivari?"

Naturally enough, I accepted this excuse for a while. But, being young, I hoped, nonetheless, that one day one of those messengers from the nobility of Europe would stop at my master's house instead of Stradivari's and order a violin from him. Some of the musicians of Cremona said that they preferred the tone of my master's instruments to those of Stradivari. But then they could not afford those of Signor Stradivari in any case, and few of them had ever played on them.

Having been then two years in my master's service, I was bold enough one day to suggest that he make better-looking instruments—take more care with the purfling, with the cutting and placement of the f-holes, and with the carving of the scrolls. Nothing could be said against his varnish. He bought it clear from a chemist and added his own colouring—gamboge for gold and powdered dragon's blood for red, and when he wished to cool the red shade to brown he added a touch of the artist's colour called Prussian blue or even occasionally a little pitch, which is not really black but an intense brown.

My master scoffed at such suggestions. Let someone commission an instrument from him for six or eight lire and then he would make a handsome violin out of the best wood and with an excellent tone, he said. But he would not waste his time or his money on such an effort without a commission.

Signor Guarneri was stubborn. He took a perverse delight in turning out instruments with a magnificent tone made of wood that Signor Stradivari would not even look at. He had a letter from a Signor Grancino, a violinmaker of Milan, who also made instruments for tavern players, asking whether he had an old gatepost he could spare, as he had to make a cello and was short of wood. My master had that letter pinned up on the wall of his workshop and delighted in pointing it out to visitors.

However, I determined to secure a commission for a good violin for my master, one he could afford to spend three months in making, instead of just a week. So one day I went to see Brother Cleophas at the Benedictine Monastery to get his help. There are, as you know, two classes of people who form a sure link between craftsmen and the nobility. The first are bankers, and the second, the clergy. It was because I knew no bankers that I went to Brother Cleophas.

I had soon told him of my master's troubles, but he was not impressed. "You had better leave matters as they are, Thomas," he said. "Even if I were able to get a commission from the Duke of Milan for a violin from Signor Guarneri, it would do him harm, not good."

"But all he needs is a little encouragement to do better work," I cried. "He says when he has been drinking that he is all alone. But I think the secret is that he feels unwanted."

Brother Cleophas shook his head. "That is impious," he said. "God wants everyone. To doubt that is to doubt God's love. In any case, Signor Guarneri is too unreliable.

Great patrons demand great pains. Signor Guarneri is incapable of taking great pains."

"He can do beautiful work and will make as handsome an instrument as Signor Stradivari if he has a commission," I insisted.

"Thomas," said Brother Cleophas seriously, "times are changing in the world—changing very fast, and all for the worse, I am afraid. The heretics have set the pattern of making master and man equal—they cannot escape that charge. That example, destructive of society as it has existed for a thousand years, is now being followed even by sons of the True Church. There is no longer an automatic submission to the nobility—no longer a strong desire on the part of the servant to please his master. Painters have been known to refuse to change a portrait to suit the sitter—who is paying for the portrait. Can you imagine that? Musicians grumble at having to sit among the servants at any great event. Soon I expect the cooks and footmen will take the same point of view. Everything is in a turmoil. I tremble at what is to come.

"Signor Guarneri has, I am afraid, the rebellious spirit of the age. Why does he not make good-looking instruments even now? Is it not because he is secretly contemptuous of those who would buy them—the nobles and kings of the land? Yes. That, I am sure, is the truth of the matter. He makes good-sounding instruments ugly in form, as if to say to the nobility, his masters, 'These are for true musicians—not for you, who only want something pretty to look at with your coat of arms on the back.'

That is not a respectful attitude, Thomas. It is not one I would dare risk recommending to the Duke of Milan."

"Father," I said, "I am sure you are mistaken. If my master had a commission from a great nobleman, he would make a beautiful violin for him. You must not forget that my master makes every violin for God. That is certainly more than making it for the Duke of Milan. And because he makes it for God, he makes sure that every violin is what it should be—a lovely singing voice which could certainly blend with those of the Seraphim around the heavenly throne."

"We taught you your theology well when you were here," said Brother Cleophas, smiling. "It is true, indeed, that it is the essence of the thing itself and not its appearance which God finds acceptable. The beggar in rags may stand closer to His throne than many kings in their finery. But we live at present not in paradise but in the world, Thomas, and the Duke of Milan takes a worldly view. He wants something that looks well in addition to sounding well.

"Think now of Signor Stradivari in contrast to your master. Signor Stradivari was brought up in different times. He learned to be submissive and humble, anxious always to please his patrons. Signor Guarneri has no such ambition. I know the man. He would resent some lacky calling on him to see how an instrument is progressing. He would refuse to accept suggestions concerning the thickness of the purfling or the throw of the scroll. Signor Guarneri is a man who will please himself before anyone else. Such men may make great artists, but they are very bad servants."

"And isn't Signor Stradivari a great artist?" I asked.

"Of course he is, my son," said Brother Cleophas. "But he has been a courtier long enough to know how to get his own way. Signor Guarneri has never had that training and would not accept it if it were offered.

"Now, how about yourself, Thomas?" Brother Cleophas continued. "You said when you were leaving us that you felt you had had a call from God to join our order and so should not leave us. Has that call come again?"

"No, Father," I said. "And to tell you the truth, it didn't come the first time. I just didn't want to leave the monastery and the whole thing was a lie."

"I understand that," said Brother Cleophas, not the slightest bit disturbed. "Indeed, I myself was guilty of the same in reverse. When I received God's call to join the Benedictines, I pretended that I had not received it, for I hated to part from my good home and my parents, whom I loved."

"Are you quite sure that you did indeed receive a call?" I asked, for I had always been bold.

"If we were quite sure of *everything*," said Brother Cleophas, "we would have no use for faith. It is faith, not certainty, that has brought man through all his difficulties. So, although I am not quite sure at all times that I received such a call, I have faith that I did what God required of me. When my end comes, I will offer Him that faith in atonement for my sins."

8

Before leaving, I asked Brother Cleophas whether I could see Annette, for although I had had scarcely a glimpse of her since leaving the orphanage, I had not forgotten her.

"Annette?" said Brother Cleophas. "Who is this Annette, pray?"

"Why, the little girl who sang the duo at the Easter Mass with me three years ago," I said. "You cannot pretend not to know her, Father. She sang like an angel. We were splendid."

"And what is her last name?" he asked.

"That I don't know," I said. "But her first name is Annette."

"I don't know whether she is still here," said the monk. "She may, like yourself, have taken service in some household. Many good families are better able to support such girls now."

"Father," I said earnestly, "please don't joke with me. She means more to me than I could ever tell you or her."

"Adam," he said, shaking his head. "Adam and Eve.

What a great deal of suffering could have been saved if the Lord in His wisdom had reflected for only a moment and arranged things differently. When you have lived as long as I, Thomas, and seen as much of the world—for we monks see a great deal—you will wonder without blasphemy whether, when the Lord took a rib of Adam and from it created Eve, He did not make His only mistake."

"Father," I said, "I am not old enough to debate such matters. May I please see Annette?"

"It is against the rules," he said. "That is one rule which cannot be broken. The girls at the orphanage may be visited only by known relatives." That was the answer I had been expecting, but the only sure loser in a contest is the one who admits his defeat, and I had a counter-argument ready.

"Then I should be allowed to see her," I said, "for you will have to admit that I am a relative, and indeed a very close one, of Annette's. We were both brought up in the same house as part of the same family, by which I mean this orphanage. We have both the same foster parents, which is to say yourself and the other brothers and sisters here. We have grown side by side through our childhood, and that is a very close relationship indeed. We both have only God as our father and Our Lady as our mother, as you yourself taught us. So may I please see her, Brother Cleophas?"

"What a pity that you were not around when Luther raised his voice," he said, smiling. "Yes, you may see her, but I will get into trouble with the Abbot."

So he told me to stay where I was (which was at the kitchen door of the monastery, for it was there I had found him) and went off and came back with Annette in her plain orphan gown, and white as a sheet with either fear or excitement.

"I will stay near," said Brother Cleophas, "to protect you from the devil, the world, and the flesh. And be quick with what you have to say in return, and protect me from my lord Abbot."

"Annette," I said, "do you remember me?"

"I have never forgotten you," she replied in a whisper.

"I am working in the town for a famous violinmaker," I said. "Someday I will be rich and come for you."

She replied, quite steadily, "I will be waiting."

"My voice has come back," I said. "People say I sing splendidly."

"I am very glad," she said.

"How are you?" I asked.

"I am very well."

There was then a very painful silence between us. There was so much I wanted to say but could not, and so much I am sure she wanted to say to me and could not. I had brought her a present and gave it to her. It was a brooch made of an ebony peg of a small viol in which I had set a few pieces of Venetian glass. I had put a pin down the back so it could be worn on the blouse.

"It's lovely," she said. "It is the very first thing I have ever had of my own."

"You have two things now," I said. "That and me." She

held out her hand to me and I took it and that was the pledge between us.

"Tut-tut," said Brother Cleophas. "None of that. The flesh, my son. The flesh." He looked anxiously around but did not part us immediately. "It is time for her to be gone now," he said. "Come, you must be gone."

"Your name?" I cried. "What is your name?"

"Occuli," she said. "Annette Occuli."

"I will come again soon," I said, and then she was gone with Brother Cleophas, leaving me both desolate and elated. When Brother Cleophas returned, I gave him a few coins which I had begged from Signora Guarneri.

"My son," he said, "give those to God's poor. From that you will get the surest blessing." So when I went past the church I put them in the poor box, which was strongly fastened to the wall and bound about with iron hoops, for alas, even in churches, people rob the poor.

Brother Cleophas was thoughtful when I took my leave. "You are very young, Thomas," he said. "Do not set your heart on Annette Occuli. She may not be for you."

"She is for no one else but me, Father," I said. He heaved a great sigh, shook his head, and so we parted.

When I had almost reached my master's workshop, the apprentice whom some years before I had punched on the nose was waiting for me. His name was Giorgio Cioppa, and he came from Rome. He was the living embodiment of that saying, known through the whole of Italy, "Good news never came from Rome." He never once made a kind remark about anybody or anything, but if anyone was guilty of an error, he was the first to spread the news. Unfortunately, he made excellent instruments.

"I hear you have made two violins," he said. "How do they sound?"

"Very poorly," I replied.

"My last violin was so good that Signor Stradivari has said I may put my label in the next one, stating that I am one of his pupils," he said.

"It surprises me that so old a man should take so great a risk," I replied, for I could not stand the beast. But he had a hide as thick as a packman's horse.

"It is no risk," he said. "Everybody agrees my instruments sound splendid. I will soon establish myself independently as a maker. Probably in Parma. There are no luthiers there, you know."

"Congratulations," I said. "I must be on my way."

"There is no need for you to hurry," he replied. "Your master is drunk again. There is nothing for you to do."

"That cannot be," I replied.

"Alas, it is so," he said. "He came to visit Signor Stradivari. He was very rude. He brought in one of his violins and almost threw it at my master. 'Even dogs must eat,' he said. 'See if you can get me ten ducats for that.' And then he cried, 'Haven't you made enough violins, old man? You say I drink too much? Well, you have a fault too. You make too many violins.' Then out he went again, lurching down the street, leaving my master so shaken he has had to go to bed."

I pushed past him to get to my master's house. There I

found everything he said was true. After a period of sobriety, my master had started drinking again, and was beyond all control.

"What started it?" I asked Signora Cattarina.

She shrugged, her face drawn and bitter. "He is a madman," she said. "The time will come when he will have to be put away."

"Oh no," I cried. "Never that."

"This time he is worse than ever," she said. "He beat the poor half-wit without mercy. And see what he has done in the workshop."

The workshop was in ruins. Every instrument he could lay his hands on was smashed, including several violins of his own which he had just finished. Some he had stamped on. Some he had smashed with one blow on his workbench.

Others, big gambas and cellos, he had flung against the wall. The destruction was the work of an enraged beast. Even the gluepot had been flung on the floor and the varnish poured over the broken instruments and tools on his workbench.

"I have to find him," I cried, and darted out into the street.

9

Signor Guarneri was not hard to find. He had been arrested by the city watch and was being held in jail on a charge of attempted murder. The magistrate who told me this, a pompous, fat man who breathed more snuff than air, for he was constantly putting a pinch of it to his nostrils, then ordered me out of his presence. I had indeed burst in on him, hearing that it was on his order that my master had been jailed. One cannot deal with people like that magistrate. They have ceased to be humans and become officials and can be reached only by lawyers.

I went to the officer of the watch of our parish and learned the details. In his drunken rage, my master had stormed out of the shop of Signor Stradivari, whom he had terribly insulted, and gone immediately to the house of a Signor Leonardo Lecchi, a musician of the Divisi and also—more important—an assistant chamberlain in the service of the Duke of Milan when he visited Cremona.

This man was notorious for not paying his bills. He had owed my master ten ducats for many months, for strings, repairs to instruments, and a new bow which Signor

Guarneri had made for him. Whenever he was asked for payment, he had some excuse for deferring the matter. He was, alas, an important man among the musicians of Cremona, one whom it was best not to offend. His importance stemmed from his position in the Duke's retinue, for whenever extra musicians were needed for some event in Cremona, it was through Signor Lecchi that they were hired.

My master had burst in on this miserable creature to demand payment for his work—payment which was long overdue. And when Signor Lecchi had not only refused payment but said that the charges made were too high, Signor Guarneri had lost control, knocked him to the ground with his fist (he was a very powerful man), and had only been saved from throttling him by others who had rushed in.

This was the story I was told, yet it was not satisfactory, for I could see no reason why my master should suddenly fly into a rage over debts so long overdue. Something else had surely happened, but what it was I could not discover then. The story did not explain, either, why my master had first burst in on Signor Stradivari waving a violin and raving at him.

The news I took back to Signora Cattarina, who immediately went to the magistrate to beg for her husband's release. And that devourer of snuff (a foreign French habit) said the charges were too serious for any bail to be considered, but moved by her pleas, he agreed that Signor Guarneri might be released to her on a bond of five hundred ducats pending his trial.

Five hundred ducats was more than she could command, even bringing in all her little loans to the raisers of silkworms, which she could not recall anyway. The house was heavily mortgaged and no further loans could be made on it. In short, the situation was hopeless. Signor Guarneri would have to remain in jail at the Duke's pleasure awaiting his trial, which might be a matter of weeks or months.

What changes can come in a few hours in men's fortunes. In the morning, when I had left to see Brother Cleophas at the monastery, hoping to help my master, all had been well. In the evening, ours was the saddest house in Cremona and the future, wherever we looked, was ruinous. There was no one to turn to. Signor Stradivari had been so insulted that although he could well afford the five hundred ducats needed to free my master, it would have been a further insult to ask him for them. Signor Bergonzi, though he had learned violinmaking side by side with my master, taught by my master's father, was not a rich man and could offer nothing but sympathy. Signor Amati, son of the great Nicolò, did nothing but repairs and was as poor as we. Signor Ruggieri could offer, with tears in his eyes, twenty ducats, no more.

"What a pity," he said, switching from grief to anger in a second, like a true son of Cremona, "that they pulled him off that dog Lecchi before he had finished the job. Lecchi owes me five ducats and Amati five more. But nobody dare press him because he is so powerful."

It was I who made the round of these violinmakers—excluding, of course, Signor Stradivari—and one positive good which resulted from it was that they agreed, between them, to repair where possible the instruments which my master had smashed in his rage.

Now I really learned what clever men violinmakers are. Truly, they could repair the world if it were smashed. They took instruments which seemed to me nothing but kindling and repaired them so well that it was hard to find where they had been broken. Seeing them restore, one by one, viols, guitars, cellos, violins which I thought beyond all hope gave me back my courage. If the violins, so badly smashed, could be restored, could not the same be done also for my master's life? What was more surprising and encouraging for me was that my own two instruments, which had not escaped the storm, after they had been repaired by Signor Amati, sounded twice as good as they did before. They did not grunt any more. They sang. I played one of them to that wretched upstart Cioppa, soon to leave Stradivari's shop. I played the opening movement of one of the concertos of Father Vivaldi of Venice, which was very popular at the time. It is in D minor, but sprightly nonetheless.

"Where did you get that instrument?" he demanded.

"Oh, it is one of those I made," I replied carelessly. "I have, as you know, been only two years as a learner."

"You told me they sounded badly," he said.

"A matter of comparison," I replied. "Think of what my violins will sound like when I have been ten years making them, like you."

Seeing how well the instruments were repaired, and

drawing from this a parable concerning Signor Guarneri, I told Signora Cattarina not to despair. "All will be well," I said. "We have only to work and keep hoping—and praying."

She was beginning to have a little fondness for me, I think. "However could so much hope come out of an orphanage?" she asked.

"Easily answered," I replied. "When you have lost everything, you are bound to start gaining something."

I had by now discovered what had triggered my master's sudden outburst of rage. He had made, some years before, a beautiful violin, perhaps as well made as one of Stradivari's, but with his own boldness in the scroll and the cutting of the f-holes. The varnish—I saw that glorious instrument later—was a glowing red-gold. It was like a sunrise. Believe me, you felt happy and warm just to look at it. The tone? No organ, not even in the greatest cathedral, had the fullness and range of that violin. I am not speaking of volume of tone. I am speaking of clarity and roundness and instancy. That violin was a masterwork. It was a violin for angels.

For whom had my master made this magnificent instrument? For whom else but that wretch Signor Leonardo Lecchi. He had promised to pay twenty-four ducats for it. He had kept it two years and then he had brought it back, that morning, while my master was out on some errand, and left it with the half-wit with a note complaining that the base bar was bad and needed to be replaced, and that the varnish was too soft and ruined the tone.

That wretch, then, had kept my master's glorious violin for two years, "trying it out," had not paid a soldo on it, and then had had the arrogance to return it, complaining that it was not well made. When Signor Guarneri got the instrument and the note, he went white with rage. He knocked poor John to the ground and smashed every instrument in sight. Then he flung out with that selfsame violin and asked Stradivari whether he couldn't sell it for him for a few ducats. He raged at Stradivari for making so many violins that other people's work could be treated with contempt. Then he sought out Signor Lecchi and beat him and, indeed, tried to kill him. So it was not just a matter of a few ducats owed. It was something far more than that—it was the arrogance and contempt of this miserable creature toward a masterpiece which had driven my master beyond control. And he was not drunk with wine but with rage.

Who is to blame him? There are many kinds of murder, after all. There is the murder of a person, which is terrible indeed. And there is the murder of a person's work, which is as bad, if not worse, but for which there is no redress.

When this story was known to the other luthiers, they petitioned the magistrate for the release of Guarneri. Signor Stradivari himself called on that fat snuff-eater to present the petition. But although Signor Stradivari was a very rich man, and although he made instruments for kings and for princes, his position was hardly to be compared with the exalted state of an assistant chamberlain to the Duke of Milan. So the petition failed.

Then Signor Stradivari offered to pay the five hundred ducats required as a bond for the release of my master. But when he heard of it, Signor Guarneri refused to be released on Stradivari's bond and indeed went into another terrible rage.

"My God," he cried, "am I to live or die at the word of Signor Stradivari—to be free or imprisoned according to his good will? Soon I will be asked to say my prayers to him. Well, I pray to God only. I accept life from His hands and death when He sends it. But I accept nothing from anyone else."

Nothing would change his mind. Mixed with his rage was hurt pride which had turned into unreasonable bitterness against the one man who could help him. And Signor Stradivari I know suffered terribly because of this. After all, he could not be blamed because his violins were always splendid and beautiful. Nor would he stop making them. True, he had no need of money. Nor were his instruments in short supply. He had at about this time ninety instruments unsold in his shop, and was particular about whom he sold them to. But to stop making instruments would have been to deprive his life of meaning. He turned them out one after another, each as carefully made as the last, his eye and hand as steady as ever, though he was now approaching ninety years of age.

He had himself suffered a heavy blow that same year with the loss of one of his sons, Alessandro, who was said to have been the most talented of his offspring. His other two sons, Francesco, who was about sixty at the time, and

Omobono, who was in his fifties, were also makers, but were completely overshadowed by their father and never put their own labels in their work. So it was not only my master who suffered from the talents and industry of Stradivari, but Stradivari's own sons as well. That is often the fate of the sons of genius.

Well, to return to the story: Since prisoners in jail had to be supported by their families, it was my job to bring Signor Guarnèri his meals, so I had plenty of opportunity of visiting with him. I brought him what cheering news I could—not much to start with, to be sure. But that heavy melancholy from which he often suffered had now taken possession of him again. For weeks I could hardly get a word out of him. He was suffering from remorse and despair. Some days he would not eat his food at all. Curiously, the half-wit John was the only person who could cheer him up.

He was allowed to visit my master on Sundays, and the poor creature, who had been so badly beaten, looked forward to his visit all week, and had to be dragged away. It was this same John, who still hated me, who finally broke through my master's gloom.

In cleaning up the workshop after all the damage which had been done, he had got together the pieces of the earthenware jar in which my master kept his varnish. (Varnish, of course, may not be kept in a metal pot, for it will dissolve some of the iron of the sides, which affects both its colour and its drying quality.) My master had smashed this pot all over his workbench, and John, instead of throwing the pieces away, had decided to mend it, though the thing was worth only a few coins.

He had no skill, and had mended it clumsily, with all the glue lines showing and some pieces in the wrong places. Still, it was all together, and on one of his visits he produced it from underneath his blouse and gave it to my master.

My master, when he saw that clumsily mended jar, broke into tears.

"Tom," he said when he had recovered, "bring me my tools tomorrow and a little wood. I must start work again." So the half-wit, who had so clumsily mended the pot, also mended my poor master.

10

The violins Signor Guarneri made in jail while awaiting trial were very rough. He had the poorest of material, for we could not afford to give him better wood, and he worked in a great hurry. There was no workbench for him, and since he was not serving a sentence but only awaiting trial, he slept in a large cell with other unfortunates—some debtors, some lunatics, some arrested on suspicion of conspiracy, and some common criminals.

In these circumstances, his tools were often stolen, he worked amid a terrible hubbub, with someone peeping over his shoulder all the time. There was no question of varnishing these instruments. As soon as he had made one, he gave it to me. It was my job to sell it immediately for whatever sum it would fetch. The scrolls were badly carved; the shape irregular. Because Signor Guarneri did not have a hot iron on which to bend the ribs, there were flat areas where there should have been smooth curves. Marvellously, however, the tone was good. That is something which cannot be explained. It surely proves that violinmaking is something more than good carpentry. But what that something is, I do not know.

All I was able to get for these violins was two or at the outside three ducats. I gave the money, on Signor Guarneri's instruction, to his wife. It was scarcely enough to support us all. He now received no money for repair work, for people would not trust their instruments to him in prison, lest they be broken by other prisoners. He still made a little money out of the sale of strings. It was plain, however hard we tried, that we would go heavily into debt unless Signor Guarneri was released from jail.

Signora Cattarina went to that wretch Lecchi, asking that he withdraw his complaint against her husband. She came back weeping. It seemed that the miserable creature was determined not only to press charges fully but to demand payment of damages in the amount of several thousand lire—damages so heavy that all Signor Guarneri's assets would have to be sold, including the house, to satisfy them.

With very little hope, I went to Brother Cleophas to plead the cause of my master, and see what help could be afforded him through Mother Church. Brother Cleophas was sympathetic but pessimistic. He undertook to have the Abbot write a letter to the Duke of Milan, asking him to help Signor Guarneri as an act of charity and mercy. But it was very doubtful whether this letter would do much good.

"After all," he said, "your master is not a well-known

maker. His instruments are not known in the court. If he were Stradivari, there would be no trouble."

There it was again. However magnificently my master's instruments sounded, they were valued at nothing because they did not all look beautiful as well. I thought of that instrument which had been the cause of the whole trouble, and told Brother Cleophas about it. Why not send that, with the letter, to the Duke? Surely, receiving the splendid violin, he could not fail to be impressed then with my master's importance. Better still, let Signora Cattarina present both the letter and the lovely violin to the Duke, and she could personally plead his cause as well.

"It might succeed," said Brother Cleophas. "I trust that Signora Cattarina has friends in Milan. She cannot expect to see the Duke the day that she arrives, you know."

"She has indeed," I said. "The Grancinos are friends of the family."

Brother Cleophas rolled his eyes upward in mock despair. "The Grancinos," he said. "Birds of a feather flock together. Let me show you some of the work of Signor Grancino." He shuffled off and returned with a tenor, covered with a bright yellow varnish, and with a big knot in the wood of the top plate. It was terribly lopsided and the gouge marks showed plainly on the roughly carved scroll.

"That is Grancino," he said. "I doubt he could make a farm cart."

"How does it sound?" I asked.

"By some miracle, magnificent," said Brother Cleophas.

I tuned it and, putting it under my chin, tried a scale in two octaves. The tone was strong, warm, and easy to produce. The C string, which on many tenors is a flabby disaster, had a burnished tone as clean as a cello's.

"What an instrument!" I exclaimed. "It is fit for a king's choir."

"Look at it," exclaimed Brother Cleophas. "It is fit for a tinker's revel and nothing more."

"Father," I said, "it seems to me that these instruments are like men. You can tell nothing about the soul from the way they look. That is why my master puts the sign of Christ in his violins—he is concerned only with the soul, not the body."

Brother Cleophas eyed me with interest. "You would have made a famous preacher," he said. "You may be one of us yet."

On this occasion I did not see Annette, but had brought a note for her, which Brother Cleophas said he would see delivered. In it I told her of our misfortune, but assured her that all would be well, and she was to save any money she could against the day of our marriage.

Signora Cattarina had still to be persuaded to make the trip to Milan. She was concerned about leaving the half-wit John, myself, and that little shadow of a girl, Celeste, while she was away. I assured her that I could manage everything, but eventually she decided that it would be better if I went with her, so as to avoid any trouble with John. Signor Bergonzi said he would keep a close eye on everything, and hearing of the plan, the aged Stradivari sent his son Francesco to live in the Guarneri house and manage things. He also wrote privately to the Duke of Milan to plead my master's cause, for he was a good and kind man.

Milan is but twenty leagues or thereabouts north and west of Cremona—two days' ride at the most, given good weather. We hired horses for the journey, for parts of the road were too bad for coaching, though carters with heavy drays made regular trips between the cities. Still, in the spring (which was when we went), there were places in the road where carts sank over their axles and two teams were needed to get them out.

I had with me a good horse pistol of Turkish make in case we were beset, but, alas, I had no opportunity to use it. It was a pity that Signora Cattarina was with me, for otherwise I could have told an excellent story of highwaymen to put Cioppa in his place when next I saw him. However, having tied up our horses first, I did fire the pistol at a tree and it made a famous noise and set my ears ringing for an hour or so afterward.

Signor Giovanni Battista Grancino and his brother Francesco were delighted to receive us when we arrived. They had heard of my master's misfortunes and were anxious to do all they could to help us, for they were very fond of him. The fact remained, however, that it was three weeks before we got an audience with His Grace the Duke, and even so, I do not think we would have seen him but for me. (Though this may seem boastful, nonetheless it is necessary to tell the truth.)

We had gone, on arrival, to the Duke's palace and handed in the letter from the Abbot. We learned that the

Duke certainly could not read it right away and we must return each day to inquire whether he had had the time to give it his attention. What was needed, the Grancinos explained, was money. A few ducats, slipped into the proper hands, would get us an early hearing; otherwise, we would have to kick our heels indefinitely in the waiting room. We did not have the ducats to spare. So we waited and waited and waited.

One day, however, in an adjoining room, we heard some singers being rehearsed in a song. There was a soprano and a tenor, and they sang both solo and in duo. The tenor, however, had been badly trained. Although he was in tune, he could not move from the chest to the head register without such a change of colour as to make a hash of the musical phrase. When, after several trials, he still failed to make this simple transition, I could bear it no more, and sang aloud the whole phrase for him, merely to demonstrate how it should be done.

The others in the waiting room turned on me those looks which are reserved for idiots and law breakers. But when the singer tried once more and again failed, all turned to me, and again I sang the phrase, which was very easy to do, for the compass was scarcely an octave. Then the door connecting the waiting room with the interior of the palace was flung open and out came a small, withered man in an old-fashioned wig of the kind called "water dog."

"Who is the singer?" he demanded in a strong French accent.

"I, signor," I replied.

He grabbed me by the arm and dragged me with no more ado out of the waiting room, along a short corridor, and into a studio across the hall. There was a low stage at one end, and a masque was being rehearsed. The withered little man went to a harpsichord at which apparently he had been playing, picked up some sheets of music, and thrust them into my hands.

"Sing it," he said. Nothing easier. I had sung from sheet music all my life. I did not even have to wait for him to give me the "ut." I sang it without trouble, and where the tenor part ended, I produced a falsetto to imitate the soprano.

"First class," said the little, withered man. "You are engaged as of this moment for the opera. What are you doing here, anyway?"

"I am trying to get my master out of prison," I replied.

"What is he in prison for?"

"Losing his temper with one of the Duke's musicians," I replied.

"Ma foi!" cried the little man. "On such a charge I would be imprisoned ten times a day. How is it possible *not* to lose one's temper with one of the Duke's musicians?"

This remark was greeted with titters, for one must always laugh at the jokes of a singing master. "Well," he continued, "we will see what we can do. Meanwhile, on with the rehearsal. You will sing tenor—with this lady."

What a beautiful creature she was—dark eyes, dark

hair, and skin as white and smooth as a snowdrift. Her name was Theresa de Matignon, and she came from Lyons, a fair town in France, though not to be compared with Cremona. We rehearsed for two hours, and since we were required at times to come close to each other and hold hands, she made a big impression on me.

We were supposed to be lovers—I a young soldier, she the daughter of a marquis whose father my father had, alas, killed in battle. My father was then sought out by her mother, who had fallen in love with him, and between the two of them they had poisoned *my* mother. But you know how these operas are—everything is a farce except the music, and the plot is only an excuse for glorious songs and choruses. The rehearsal continued for two hours and at the end of that time all were told to meet again at ten in the morning to rehearse once more. The little, withered Frenchman, without another glance at me, gathered up his music and was about to disappear into the interior of the palace when I stopped him.

"Signor," I said, "what about my master?"

"Forget him," he said in a great hurry. "You have a new master—the Duke of Milan."

"That's not possible," I said. "I came here to get my master out of jail."

"My friend," said the Frenchman, "you are young. I am old. Let me give you a piece of good advice. When someone is in trouble, attend to your own affairs. If they get out of their trouble, rush to congratulate them, and you will soon be friends again. In short, young man, don't borrow trouble. You have enough of your own without meddling in that of others."

"In that case, signor," I said, "I cannot help you in your trouble."

"My trouble!" he cried. "Young man, what trouble am I in?"

"You have a work to prepare for the Duke and you haven't a tenor. I judge you have only a few days left in which to prepare it."

"Young man," said the Frenchman, "I can get fifty tenors right here in Milan by merely snapping my fingers."

"Then why put up with that donkey you had braying before I arrived?" I asked.

He sighed. "It is true that God has never visited Lombardy," he said, repeating an old adage. "All right," he continued, "I admit it. There is a shortage of tenors. They are all singing in Venice or Rome or Paris. So I have helped you by offering you the post."

"And I have helped you by accepting it—provided you help my master."

In the end, I got him to agree to speak to the Duke about my master and see whether he would not grant an interview to Signora Cattarina.

Even so, it was a week before that interview could be arranged. However, matters went much better than we could have hoped for. Signora Cattarina, having stated her case, stressed the importance of her husband as a luthier. And producing the glorious violin as a gift for the Duke, she said that it was the very instrument which

Signor Lecchi had returned, complaining about the tone after keeping it for two years. The singing master, M. Verville, was present at this interview, since I was his client. When the instrument was uncovered, his eyes sparkled.

"What do you think?" said the Duke.

The singing master took it and played a few passages—badly, I thought.

"Marvellous," he said. "Just the instrument for your first violinist. It is magnificent."

"Would you keep such an instrument and send it back after two years, saying the tone was poor?" asked the Duke.

"Never, as I fear the justice of God," said M. Verville.

That decided it. The Duke ordered Signor Guarneri to be released and all charges against him dropped. A little later, having received a letter from the Duke dismissing him from his service, Signor Lecchi departed from Cremona without a word to a soul, but leaving behind him a great number of debts, which are unpaid to this day.

11

I now entered the service of the Duke of Milan, moving from the top of Signor Guarneri's house, where my companions were pigeons and old lumber, to a little cubbyhole in the Duke's palace which I shared with a potboy and a running footman—that is to say, a man who travelled on the back of the Duke's coach and was required to run up to the door immediately it stopped, in order to let His Grace and his lady dismount.

I was sorry to leave Signor Guarneri, who would now be without anyone to help him. But the choice was not mine or his—when the Duke commanded, he had to be obeyed; the more so since he had obtained the release of my master from jail and the dismissal of charges against him.

Signor Guarneri was sorry to have me go. He was not an affectionate man, but given to brooding and days of silence when he pondered some dark problem of his mind. It was only when things were going exceptionally well that he became that other person—charming, gay, vital, and handsome.

"If there is any trouble, come back here," he said. "I will always be willing to help you. But the fact is you would never make a violinmaker, and your talent is in singing. You have an excellent ear. It is much better for you to enter the Duke's service."

Signora Cattarina, out of the small capital that she had managed to retain, got me a good secondhand suit which she made almost new by turning the cloth inside out. The little shadow of a girl, Celeste, broke into tears at my leaving, though for what reason I do not know. The only one who was truly glad to have me out of the house was John, who, when I was standing at the door with my bag on the morning of departure, pushed me out, muttering loudly all the while.

I was given a free pass to ride with a carter to Milan, a grizzled old fellow who had lost an eye in the Austrian wars. The same pike thrust which had destroyed his sight had torn away half his face, which was all pulled to one side. He had a stub of clay pipe in his mouth, turned upside down, out of habit, against the rain, and in it he smoked a very rank tobacco which made the smell of the sweat of his horse pleasant by comparison.

He had fought in a lot of battles and had killed a lot of men, he said, but how many he did not know. "They fire. We fall down. We fire. They fall down. That is the way it is in a battle. Then the cavalry charge and the pikemen come on. Ten years I was in it."

"What was it all about?" I asked to get his reaction.

"Why, who was to be King of Austria and who was to be King of Spain," he said.

"And who finally became king?" I asked to test him.

"I don't know," he said. "But I will tell you this—whoever sits on the throne of Spain or the throne of Austria or the throne of Poland for that matter, I sit on this cart and that is good enough for me."

Learning that I was going to the Duke's palace to be a singer, he asked me to sing for him, but was not much impressed, despite the purity of my voice.

"That would get you nowhere in the army," he said. "Your singing may be good enough for a duke, but no soldier would listen to it for a minute. Do you know 'The Breakfast of Prince Eugene'?"

I did not, and he sang it to me, in a cracked monotone, roaring out the chorus a fourth higher, but without any tune I could discover. The words were not fitting for Christian ears. However, I told him it was a fine song, and he sang two or three more of the same kind, and then, handing me the reins, got back into his cart among the goods he was carrying, and fell asleep.

When I parted with him, he told me he left Milan for Cremona each Friday. I would find him outside the Church of St. Gregory at noon. "You won't last long with the Duke, singing the way you do," he said, shaking his head. "You'll need a ride back."

Actually, I hardly ever saw the Duke. He was a very small man for a duke, with a large nose like a carrot sticking out of his face. He had a silver-mounted cane and thumped out the time on the floor with this all through the opera. I was warned to sing to *his* time and not that of our French singing master, M. Verville. The singing, then, was not a great success, but the costuming and the lights were much admired.

From then on, I fell into a routine of singing and violin playing and general music study which occupied most of my time. We musicians had always to be available in the evening until the Duke retired, and those who did not live in the palace were often kept up yawning until one or two in the morning lest the Duke take it into his head to hear something sung or played.

He gambled at cards a great deal and liked to have several musicians playing softly while he did so. When he won, he sometimes rewarded them handsomely. But when he was losing, he cursed them for "noisy dogs." To tell the truth, he had no more music in him than my friend the carter and would slap his cards down on the table with the greatest noise during the most delicate passages.

All in all, things went very well for me at the Duke's court. I was given my board and keep and three ducats a month as a musician, which, alas, were often stolen from me by the running footman whose room I shared. No matter where I hid the money, he would find it and steal it. He was quite brazen about it and said that I owed him something for sharing his room. There was nothing I could do about this, and the potboy sided with the footman in the matter.

I soon found that servants can be more tyrannous to each other than their masters. The new servant—and as a musician I was, of course, a servant—had no friends and no one, then, to take his side. So I got permission from M. Verville to take up lodgings with the Grancinos, who were glad to have me, and I did not miss the ducat a month which I paid to them for my room and board. There were a great number of Grancinos in Milan, all instrument makers, and they all loved the Christian name Giovanni. They all lived around the Contrada Larga and were in and out of each other's premises all the time. They were quite the opposite of the Guarneris.

My old master had a brother in Venice and a father who lived somewhere in Cremona, as I have said, but they never saw each other. The Grancinos, on the other hand, could not live out of each other's sight. They were open-handed, talkative, great gossips, and careless. The ancestor of the family, Paolo, had been a pupil of the great Nicolò Amati at the same time as Signor Stradivari. Paolo Grancino was now dead, of course. His instruments, of which I saw several, followed the Amati style but only loosely.

No Grancino it seemed could take care with anything. Yet the tone of all their instruments was surprisingly good; not as good as my old master's, not at all, but sweet and smooth. One Grancino would cheerfully finish the instrument of his brother if the brother wanted to go away for a while. If they were in a hurry with a violin or a cello, they left out the purfling, which I have explained is the thin inlay of boxwood put around the edges of the top and bottom to prevent splitting. Instead of this inlay, which took time to insert and mitre at the corners, they just drew a line in black ink around the edge of their instrument.

"Who cares?" they would say. "One does not, after all, play the purfling."

Working as loosely as they did, they used any wood that came their way, provided it had good acoustic qualities. Francesco made the back of a viola out of three pieces of poplar with the flame of the wood not even matching. I shook my head at this carelessness.

"The rogue who buys it will probably sit on it or throw it at his wife in a year," said Francesco with a laugh.

But the Grancinos were by no means the worst violin-makers in Milan. They were matched and even outstripped by the family of Testore, outside of whose shop there hung a signboard showing an eagle. That is hardly a bird noted for the beauty of its song, but it seems that at one time a family whose crest had been that of the eagle had occupied that house. Anyway, the Testores made even worse-looking instruments than the easygoing, generous Grancinos. Their selection of wood was just as bad, and their varnish was worse, for they mixed into it substances called siccatives which dried the varnish fast but gave it a flat look when dry.

"If it is Monday and you want a new violin by Tuesday, go to Testore. If it is Monday and you want a new violin by Friday, go to Grancino." That is what one of the musicians in the Duke's band told me, discussing these makers.

My old master, Signor Guarneri, never made a violin as

carelessly as either the Grancinos or the Testores—omitting for the moment those he made in prison. He could, as you have seen, make beautiful instruments but was crowded out of that market by Signor Stradivari. So he made something in between.

As for the tone of his instruments, there was so much more power, so much more colour and majesty in them, that they were not to be compared with anyone else's. That violin of his which was given to the Duke and which had now been handed to Guglielmo Viotti, who was leader of the Duke's band, had immediately asserted its superiority over all the instruments in the string choir. People commented on the difference, but in their ignorance thought that Viotti's playing had improved. Not at all. His playing was the same. But my old master's wonderful violin permitted him to produce varieties of sound impossible on the Austrian Stainer violin which he had previously played. Signor Viotti sold the Stainer. He got forty lire for it. Yet Signor Guarneri had not been able to get twelve for the instrument that replaced it.

Now I learned from the Grancinos something more about my old master, and the reason for his black moods and sudden bouts of temper, depression, and drunkenness. His life, as he saw it, had been doomed from the day of his birth—doomed by his father, whom he now never saw. This is the story.

My master's father was Joseph Guarneri. He, the father, had a brother, Peter, both the sons of Andrea Guarneri. They had all lived in the same house in Cremona and the two sons had been taught violinmaking by Andrea.

Peter, the oldest, as soon as he was of age, left his father's house in Cremona, married, and set up business in Mantua at the court of the duke there. He was fond of the gay life of the court, lived from one excitement to another, and was a favourite of the duke, who saw he had plenty of patronage. He grew rich, both as a player and teacher and as a maker of instruments. His life was all pleasure and very few worries.

The younger brother, Joseph, was left at home. He also wanted a gay life at some ducal court. But on him fell the responsibility of helping his father, Andrea. He had to remain in Cremona, making instruments, keeping books, waiting on customers. He married, but that did not set him free but only increased his responsibilities. The father's business fell off, and the son, Joseph, had to work harder. Money was borrowed on the house and a message sent to the other son in Mantua, asking him to help. The son did not even reply. When Andrea died, then, his son Joseph's life had been limited to what was available in Cremona, which, having no court, had little to offer the musician outside of playing in churches. Joseph was the main beneficiary under his father's will, but he inherited his father's debts too.

What had occurred in the Guarneri family in one generation was now repeated exactly in the second. Joseph Guarneri also had two sons. Again the elder was called Peter and the second Joseph, or Giuseppe—that being the man who was my master. Again the elder, Peter, left home when he could, but instead of going to Mantua, he went to Venice. Again this second Peter Guarneri found there in the court of the Doge of Venice the excitement, the glamour, the opportunities, and the riches which his uncle had found at Mantua.

My master, the second son, was left in Cremona to help his father. The father had inherited debts from his father. His son Peter, in Venice, did nothing to reduce them. He remained in Venice, married, happy, and the father of a number of children, none of whom ever visited Cremona, though the distance was not great. He became famous and wealthy, as much sought as a player of violin as he was as a maker of instruments. Meanwhile, my old master had to remain in Cremona.

Discouraged by the weight of his debts and the competition from Signor Stradivari, Joseph Guarneri, my old master's father, at last gave up and stopped making instruments entirely. For a while he repaired them. Then he took to gambling, and feeling that he had been cheated out of his life by his more fortunate brother, he neglected his home and his wife and took up with other women. The full load of the household fell on my old master. He had to support his father and his mother, who were soon separated. His father had an illegitimate son, who had been born a half-wit and sent to an asylum to be trained into some kind of sense by a plain diet and severe discipline, for no other kind of treatment is known for such people. When my master heard of this, he went immediately to the asylum to see his half brother, and pitying him, he took him out to care for in his own home. That was the creature John. Plainly, the reason John had taken such a dislike to me on sight was that he was of the opinion that I would oust him from the house, sending him back to the miseries of the asylum.

All this I learned from the Grancinos. I now understood Signor Guarneri far better than I had before. No wonder he had such black moods, such fits of drunkenness. His life had been taken from him. What a success he could have made, handsome as he was, in some court with a powerful patron to ensure his fortune. But everything had been ruined from the outset.

"Don't pity him too much," said Carlo Grancino, one of the clan, who was more serious than the others. "His name may not shine now. But it will blaze brightly when we are all forgotten. No man makes such violins as he. Compared with his work, all we make here are boxes."

"What a pity he should be so little known and appreciated now," I said.

"Success makes Stradivari greater," said Carlo. "It would ruin Guarneri. Men are like horses. Some respond to pats and coaxing. But there are other great ones who need the boot and the spur."

12

Signor Guarneri's misfortune had (by God's marvellous design, as Brother Cleophas said) opened up my whole life for me. The warmhearted Grancinos were a welcome change from the gloomy Guarneri household. I received many compliments upon my singing and was invited to some of the best houses in Milan to sing at social events. To be sure, I was a servant and not a guest. Yet some of these great people spoke to me with interest and affection, and at one house, that of the da Nobrigas, I was treated almost as a son. Childless themselves, they invited me often to their lovely mansion on the northern outskirts of Milan to sing while Signora da Nobriga played on a large harpsichord. Sometimes I played violin, and you may be sure that I recommended to them when I could the instruments of Signor Guarneri. But their interest was not in instruments but in me and my singing, so I could not get them to place an order with him, and a certain delicacy prevented me pressing the matter too much.

Meanwhile, at the Duke's court, my fame brought me many favours. I received a new wardrobe of handsome suits and linen. I was called upon to sing in more and more roles, and often a performance was interrupted while the audience applauded my rendering of an aria. Occasionally—when a performance had been given in honour of someone's birthday or saint's day—I received a little purse with a few coins. Within a year of joining the Duke's court, I was a person of some substance, envied by some of my fellow musicians and flattered by others. I also became a favourite with the Duke. He had no ear for music, of course. But the fame I brought to his musical evenings reflected on himself, adding to his own lustre.

He now thumped all the harder on the floor with his silver-mounted cane, as if this thumping of his was responsible for the success of his musical evenings. Sometimes, if he had taken a little too much wine, he would try to join in and sing with me or one of the other singers. His voice was as bad as that of the carter who had brought me from Cremona, and if any of the guests dared to say "Hush," he would turn around and say, "Damme, I'll sing if I want. I own every man jack of them, and every note they utter"—which was certainly the truth of the matter.

He was a stern and forthright man, and yet just. It is stated that at the siege of Cremona in 1702 he had been unfortunate enough to be standing between two cannon when they were both discharged in the same moment. That had ruined what ear for music he ever possessed. Certainly he liked loud pieces, and I do not think he heard the tenderer passages, during which he often fell asleep.

Among my admirers was Theresa de Matignon, the

French girl whose dark hair, dark eyes, and snowdrift skin made my heart jump whenever I saw her. She was, I think (for one did not discuss these matters), a year or two older than I. She had a quick, bright nature, like a bird, a voice of lovely purity and great range, and a quick wit. Our many rehearsals and performances meant that we spent a great deal of time together, though always in public. Still, we had a few moments of semi-privacy and her nature was so attractive and understanding that I had soon told her the whole of my story, not leaving out my love for Annette, whom I was one day going to marry.

"And so you should," she said, "and rescue her from that dreadful place. Perhaps the Duke could be persuaded to add her to his band of musicians, since she sings so beautifully. You should speak to M. Verville about that."

How odd it is that when she made that suggestion I should have felt my very first doubt concerning Annette! Oh, it was no great doubt—just a lack of the usual elation at the prospect of marrying her. And when, once or twice in the weeks that followed, Theresa again mentioned this suggestion of hers, I found that I really didn't want Annette to join the Duke's court, and indeed became a little annoyed at the idea.

Meanwhile, Theresa was very understanding, and being the only friend I had of my own age, she was able to give me the kind of advice I could trust. When I mentioned the tiny changes of feeling I was having toward Annette, she comforted me immediately. "You must not reprimand yourself," she said. "And you mustn't make yourself do as a man what you thought you wanted to do as a child. After all, you are almost fully grown now. Many things have changed since you sang together at the Mass so long ago. Don't forget, she may have changed too, and her own feelings about you may not be so fervent."

That came as a shock. Indeed, I felt betrayed on the moment. It was understandable that my feelings might change a little toward Annette. But it was intolerable that her feelings should change toward me. In any case, I took more and more pleasure in Theresa's company. She had, it is true, exalted ideas about the importance of France, and once ventured to suggest that the singers of Normandy were possibly the equal of those of Lombardy.

But one has to expect a certain amount of nonsense from girls, who are not given the same sense and steadiness of judgment as boys. And when I laughed at the very idea, she laughed too, so I could see that she was making a joke. Then she added, wittily, "Of course, we have no one in Normandy who can match the musical talent of our noble patron, the Duke of Milan." That was such an excellent joke that we both laughed heartily together, but later, when I was alone, I wondered whether she had not, after all, been mocking our Italian singers.

Now I began to realize that when two young people sing together it is a form of courtship. Something not expressed in words flows between them—there is an interchange of their persons also. This had happened with me and Annette, and now it happened again (there being far more opportunity for it) with Theresa. No one is to be blamed for this. You cannot sing without emotion. The purer the emotion, the better the singing. That is true even if occasionally a note is false. How then can you sing of love and not fall in love? It cannot be done. And when the harmonies were perfect between us, it seemed to me that we were one indeed and must remain so forever.

I brought Theresa to the Grancino house to meet them, and although they were as warm and outgoing with her as they were with everyone else, I sensed that they did not entirely like her. That was a surprise. She was very witty and gracious with them, and offered to help with the dinner, though she was wearing one of her best gowns. It was agreed that she would only soil her dress and so she sat aside singing little snatches of madrigals and other songs, very prettily, accompanying herself on a lute. They all agreed she sang beautifully. But when she left I felt that there had been something missing from the visit, though I could not decide what it was.

Brother Cleophas, visiting Milan on some business concerning the purchase of cloth—Milan being a famous centre of the clothing trade—grew very quiet when I introduced him to Theresa. Then he fetched so many deep sighs that I decided he was meditating again on the devil, the world, and the flesh. He took me aside and gave me a little package. "Annette has sent this for you," he said. "You remember her? Her last name is Occuli." I put the package aside, not wishing to open it immediately in his presence.

"You have any message for her?" he asked.

"Certainly. Tell her I am well and I think of her often."

"Often?" he said. "It used to be always. Aren't you going to open the package?"

"I will open it later," I replied.

"Well, have you nothing to send back with me?" he asked.

"Certainly," I said, and going to the strongbox where I kept my money—I had now quite a store—I gave him three ducats.

"What's this for?" he asked.

"For the poor," I replied.

"In that case, I think you had better keep it for yourself," he said slowly. "For you are poorer now than you have ever been in all your life."

"What a ridiculous thing to say," I said. "I am richer than I have ever been. Soon I will have enough put by to get married." Those words came out of my mouth without thinking. I was just offended at Brother Cleophas insisting that I was poor when I had earned so much with my singing.

"Am I to tell that to Annette?" he asked.

"No," I replied. "I will tell her myself when I am ready."

"I will say a Mass for you on All Hallows Eve," he said. "When we pray for lost souls." And off he went.

To tell the truth, between rehearsals with Theresa and practice and other needed activities, I forgot all about Annette's package for several days. When I opened it, I found it contained a handkerchief of finest linen with our initials embroidered in blue and gold silk thread in one corner. With it was a note saying very little about herself except that she was well, but full of concern and questions about me.

Though I was happy to get the handkerchief, the embroidered initials irritated me and her letter seemed foolish and childish and I put it aside. I thought more and more about Theresa's sensible advice—not to be bound in my young manhood by the desires and decisions of my childhood. Besides, I was daily becoming more and more attracted to Theresa herself. So, to make everything honest, I at last summoned up my courage and wrote a note to Annette saying that my feelings toward her had changed and, while I hoped she would always look on me as a friend, it would be wrong for me to marry her, for my heart belonged to someone else.

When I had sent that letter off by safe hand to Cremona, I immediately regretted writing it. But I steeled myself not to send another, apologizing. I argued that the letter, hurtful as it would be to Annette, was nonetheless sensible and honest. In a little while I received her reply. Not one written word. Only the decorated viol peg which I had given her years ago as a pledge of my love.

It hurt to get that back. I couldn't throw it away. I couldn't keep it. In the end I confided everything to Signora da Nobriga, and gave her the brooch.

"I will keep it, Tom," she said. "If you should want it back, it will be here."

"Signora," I cried, "why am I so faithless? I have

thrown aside Annette and I have never gone back to see Signor Guarneri since I left his house. Nor have I ever returned to the monastery to visit the monks who were so kind to me."

"I don't think you are truly faithless, Tom," she replied. "But there is a time in everybody's life, which comes sooner or later, when they are so busy growing that they concentrate on themselves, and have nothing left over to spare for others. It is a very dangerous time," she added. I had been singing for her when this conversation took place, and she had served me with a dish of tea. I did not like it at all, but it was the English fashion, much admired among the nobility of Lombardy, and she tried to keep up with these things.

"What is dangerous about it?" I asked.

"Some people never get through that period. Like children, they concentrate all their lives on their own happiness and what they want for themselves. Most people, however, come to realize that they cannot be truly happy unless they do something for others. Happiness can never come from selfishness. Your beautiful voice is wasted unless it is heard by others. You have to give your voice to people. It is the same with our lives."

Now this was much the same kind of thing that I had heard from the monks at the monastery, and it certainly struck me as strange that the old but wealthy Signora da Nobriga should have the same point of view as the Brothers at the monastery, who were very poor. But then she could talk about giving because she had plenty to give. And they could talk about giving because they were always receiving. With me it seemed the case was very different. What I had I had earned myself, and wasn't I supposed, after all, to look after myself before anybody else?

Nonetheless, I did not feel comfortable about Annette. I told Theresa what I had done and she said I had acted very wisely in setting her free. She was the only one I felt entirely at home with, and a few months later I bought her a little silver ring with two amethysts set in it.

Alas, about this time another young man joined the Duke's court as a musician. He was very dark and small and had curly hair. But he played the flute as well as a blackbird sings. I must say that for him. Nonetheless, he was quite ugly, and I rather pitied him. Imagine my surprise, then, to find him and Theresa one day in deep conversation together. I told myself they were just talking over part of the score where she, playing the part of a princess turned into a bird, had to answer the flute, played by her lover, who had come searching for her through the woods.

But I then began to notice how often they had to have these earnest conversations, and how much more animated she was in talking to this young man, Marco, who came from Sicily, than she was in talking with me. Later still, I noticed that my little amethyst ring was no longer on her finger, and when I asked her about it, she said, casually, that she had mislaid it somewhere but undoubtedly it would turn up.

It was very strange. Only a few weeks after I had parted with Annette, Theresa became less interested in me, and soon had eyes only for the Sicilian. Pride prevented me from mentioning this to anybody, but I felt very wretched and wondered what I had done to lose Theresa's favour.

I tried being even more pleasant to her, more attentive, and buying her little surprises. But this, instead of softening her, made her all the more cool toward me. Once, when we had to rehearse together, she kept me waiting an hour and a half before she turned up, and when our parts did not go well together, it was I who had to take the blame from M. Verville. When this happened again, and I was once more blamed, I said indignantly that I had been willing to rehearse but Signorina de Matignon had been delayed several times and so we had not had enough practice together.

"My friend," said M. Verville with a half grin on his old face. "Haven't you yet learned that to sing tenor you have to discipline the soprano?"

In the end, when Theresa, infatuated with her flute player (a silly instrument which can be played by every farm boy in Italy), neglected me and our rehearsals more and more, I decided to teach her a lesson. So, in one of our duets, sung a cappella, or without instrumental support, I deliberately transposed my part a third higher. This, though it provided me with difficulties in the upper registers, put her own high notes beyond her reach. Her voice faltered, strained, and cracked, and she fled in confusion from the stage. M. Verville, in the prompter's box, immediately tumbled to what I was doing. When I glanced at him, he was pretending to examine the score, but smiling nonetheless.

Thereafter, Signorina de Matignon did not miss any rehearsals. But all was over between us. Strangely, however, we sang together as beautifully as ever. Thus I learned that I did not have to fall in love with every pretty girl who sang a duet with me. I wish I had learned it before.

13

For a long time, busy with my own affairs, I determined after my encounter with Theresa to follow Brother Cleophas's advice and have nothing more to do with the devil, the world, and the flesh but stick entirely to my music. One day I happened to see the old carter who had brought me from Cremona to Milan. He was seated on his cart outside the Church of St. Gregory, waiting for a load, with his pipe thrust into his mouth upside down, as usual, as a defence against the wind and the rain.

I went over to him, thinking to boast a little of how well I had done with my singing, when he had been so sure that the Duke of Milan would soon throw me out in the street. He did not recognize me in my fine clothes. Of course I had grown, for it was now almost three years since I had left Cremona. Also, I think he was losing his wits, through being so long alone with only his horse for company. But when I at last got him to realize who I was, he looked me over and cast around in his mind for some wise remark to make to me.

"Easy come, easy go," he said, shaking his head. "Remember, I can always give you a ride back to Cremona. But it will cost you seventy soldi."

"Thank you," I replied. "I will certainly bear that in mind if I need to go back."

He leaned forward to spit on the ground between the shaft of the cart and the horse. He did this with great judgment, as if it were a particular gift of his, not given to others.

"So you are a singer," he said. "Well, you should learn to play an instrument. A voice is soon gone. Mine remains, thanks be to God. But one day it will go and then I will be able to amuse myself on the flute."

His voice, of course, if he had ever had any, had gone long before. But I did not say so, contenting myself with remarking that I could already play an instrument, namely the violin.

"Is that so?" he exclaimed. "You are a talented young fellow, in truth. And it so happens I can do you a favour. You are very fortunate to have found me here."

"Oh?" I said. "And what favour can you do me?"

He reached around behind him and picked up a very big sack. It was bulging with goods, but seemed very light, for he could manage it with one hand. He put it between his legs, the bottom resting against the buttocks of the horse, and proceeded to undo the top.

"I have something here I don't show to everybody," he said. "But since you are a particular friend of mine and a musician as well, I will show it to you. There," he said, flinging open the mouth of the sack. "See for yourself. And every one of them a bargain."

I peered into the sack. It was stuffed with string instruments—guitars, lutes, viols, violins, all thrust in higgledy-piggledy, jammed into each other so that the bridges of many of them had fallen down, and some were cracked.

"Take your pick," he said. "Any one you fancy for just two ducats."

"Where did you get these?" I asked.

"Cremona," he said.

"Who from?"

"The madman."

"What madman?"

"Guarneri—who else? He needs money." He put his thumb, stretched out stiff from the palm of his hand, into his mouth—a gesture we in Lombardy use to indicate someone drinking wine. He gave me a big wink. "Food—everyone can afford," he said. "Wine—nobody can afford."

I fumbled through the sack and took out a violin. It was one of my old master's. I could recognize it immediately—the f-holes with the pointed extremities, and shortened corners of the bouts, the scroll carved with such impatience.

"How many of these do you have?" I asked.

"See for yourself. But if you take my advice, you will buy the lutes or the gambas. They are much prettier."

I found three violins.

"How long will you be here?" I asked.

"I leave as soon as they bring me the cowhides from the

tanners there," he replied, pointing up a dark alley beside the church, where the tannery was situated. (Because of the closeness of the tan yard, it was held, bodies buried in the Church of St. Gregory would never molder away.)

"Don't leave until I get back," I replied. "I will buy these fiddles." Off I dashed to the Contrada Larga to the Grancino house, where, without a word to a soul, I flew into my room, opened my strongbox, and took out twelve ducats. Then I returned and handed them to the carter.

"Three of these are for you," I said. "The rest you are to give to Signora Cattarina, wife of Signor Guarneri. Say they are in payment for three violins. Do not say who bought the violins."

He looked suspiciously around the square, and then reached again into the back of the cart and put a big cudgel on the seat beside him. "What a fool you are," he growled. "You would never have made a soldier. To hand me money like this in broad daylight! Why couldn't you have taken me up the alley to give it to me?"

"Nonsense," I said. "You will be perfectly safe."

"Bah," he snorted. "I do not know how you lived so long with your throat uncut. You are a danger to your fellow men." Not a word of thanks for the money from the grumpy old rascal.

"Be sure to give the nine ducats to Signora Cattarina and just keep three for yourself," I warned, distrusting his surly attitude.

"If I don't, what could you do about it?" he demanded. "Let me tell you something. You are a fool. And it is only the result of the luck of a fool that you are dealing with the only honest carter in Milan."

"Not such a fool as you think," I replied. "Remember, I am a member of the court of the Duke. And if you steal my money, you will pay heavily for it."

"The Duke," he said. "Perhaps I know him better than you, my young cockerel. For I played in his choir with cannon for an instrument once."

A little later, his load of hides having arrived, he shifted the bag of instruments to the seat beside him, and went off, glancing around him first to see if anyone noted his departure.

I took the three violins back to the Grancino house and explained how I had come by them. Carlo, who, as I have said, was the more thoughtful of that happy Grancino tribe, was sad. "Why should so great a man have so terrible an affliction?" he asked. "It is a kind of insanity."

His wife was inclined to be stern. "He has only to stop drinking and dwelling on his miseries," she said. "Self-pity is at the bottom of it all."

"No," said Carlo. "It is much more than that. I don't know what it is. But it is something none of us here have ever felt—thanks be to God and all His saints."

"It is a kind of loneliness," I said, and recounted how, when I first came to Signor Guarneri's house and he had fallen victim to one of these bouts, I had found him wandering by the river and asked him whether he was sick. His reply had been, "Sick? It is worse than that. I am alone. Always alone."

"How can he be alone, with his wife, his half brother John, and that girl Celeste in his household?" demanded Signora Grancino. "Right next door is Bergonzi, who I know is a very kind man, and next to him Signor Stradivari, who will help anyone and loves to talk about instruments. So how can he be alone?"

"Sometimes I feel alone myself," said Carlo.

"You?" she demanded.

"Yes. Me. I don't know why it is. It is as if I was separated from something beautiful and could not find my way back to it."

"Fifteen years we are married and you come up with something new every week," said his wife.

But I think I understood what Carlo was saying, for I sometimes had the same feeling. Once, standing in the monastery church when I was a boy, watching the lovely colours made on one of the old grey pillars by the light streaming through a stained-glass window, I had felt such a sense of yearning and loss that I had almost cried out. Perhaps that feeling was with Guarneri all the time—the feeling of separation from loveliness, or perhaps the feeling that all beauty lasts only for a moment, as the colours of the stained-glass window dissolved into darkness when the sun set.

That evening I looked over the three violins my master had made. The Grancinos crowded around, examining the instruments. I pictured him sitting alone now in that workshop, working on the corner blocks or gouging out the top or back. Hour after hour he would work, never saying a word, until he was called away to eat. Yes, he was very lonely indeed.

We strung the instruments up and played a concerto written by Father Vivaldi for four violins. How well my old master's instruments sang. We played until the womenfolk complained we were wasting too many candles and must go to bed. While I lay in bed, I thought of my old master alone in his workshop, haunted by the devil of solitude, and my heart went out to him.

14

About this time Signor Stradivari died. His death came as a great blow. To be sure, he was about ninety years of age, maybe more. But year after year he had continued working, without the slightest trace of change. He was seldom ill. His eyesight seemed as sure as ever. His hand grew a little unsteady, but the last violins he made showed little sign of age. He worked to the last day of his life, supervising everything in his studio. His son Omobono told me that the day before he died he had inquired for a supply of fresh glue, fearing that the glue they were using was losing its power through being heated too many times.

When he died, that one person whom we had all looked upon for so long as a fixture in a changing world was no longer with us. We felt, all of us, sadder for that. We all went to Cremona for his funeral. The Grancinos came, and many musicians from the court of the Duke of Milan. Bergonzi, Amati's son, Ruggieri—all were present, and I as well.

There was no music at the funeral Mass, of course. But when the body had been placed in the sepulchre in the Chapel of the Holy Rosary in the Church of St. Dominic, then all those musicians gathered in the chapel and played a beautiful arrangement of the Credo from a Mass by Palestrina. It was agreed that this was entirely fitting, for all his life Stradivari had been, above all things, a believer in God, and in the mercy of our resurrection from the dead. When our tribute was over and we left to gather in the Stradivari home and console the widow and her sons, Signor Guarneri remained in the church. An hour later he had not returned and Signora Cattarina asked me to get him. He was seated in the gathering gloom in the chapel, by the tomb of Stradivari, which was heaped high with flowers.

"Master," I whispered, "come away now. Signora Cattarina is anxious for you."

"I do not want to leave him alone," he said.

"Signor," I replied, "he has the company of God's angels and saints at this moment."

He looked at me very strangely and asked solemnly, "Thomas, is it really true that life is death and death is life?" For such a strange question I had no answer.

Having obtained permission from M. Verville, I stayed that week with my old master. John the half-wit was not at all happy to see me back. Many times, seeing me at the door, he tried to push me out, but I understood him now and was patient with him. The little mouse-like girl, Celeste, had grown greatly. Indeed, she was almost a woman, and quite pretty. I had thought she would show some interest in me, for certainly I had grown too, and people said I was handsome. It had been remarked in my hearing on one or two occasions that I had a "manly appearance," and I took the opportunity when she was around to sing a bar or two from some aria, so she could appreciate the quality of my voice, which was certainly of the best.

But, incredible as it seems, she had eyes only for that miserable former apprentice of Signor Stradivari's, Cioppa. I could not believe her lack of taste. They were to be married that autumn, and when I heard this, and offered her, somewhat coldly, my congratulations, she beamed with pleasure at the prospect and, blushing, said that Cioppa was the kindest and truest man she had ever met. Plainly, there is no accounting for the blindness of women.

I had a serious talk with Signora Cattarina and my old master. Things were in a very bad way with them. Business had fallen off and they were now compelled to live to a large extent from Signora Cattarina's investments in the silk trade. Indeed, one of the sons of Stradivari, Paolo, had entered the cloth trade rather than follow his father into the art of violinmaking. There was no great demand for violins any more.

Signor Stradivari had left several dozen instruments finished, some varnished and some not, and if it was not for the great wealth the father amassed, the family would have found themselves in straightened circumstances now. "The demand for Cremona violins is past its peak," said Omobono, shaking his gray head. Although the youngest of Signor Stradivari's sons by his first wife, he was already an old man. "The French, the Dutch, and the Tyrolese are making instruments. Even the English lutemakers are turning out violins. Soon nobody will care for the instruments of my father."

"That's impossible," I said. "Such splendid instruments will always be wanted."

Omobono hardly resembled his father at all, but took after his mother. He was slow to speak, and I thought rather dull of mind. Yet he had a fund of plain sense.

"Thomas," he said. "Great art demands powerful patrons who can pay great sums of money for it. There are dukes and kings and counts in plenty still. But the recent wars have impoverished them. They have no money left to patronize the arts. As for musicians, surely you know how poor and insecure they are. They cannot afford to lay out large sums for instruments. Anything will do, since they play ensemble.

"The world is upside down, Thomas. There are silk merchants in Milan who have more money than His Grace the Duke. But silk merchants, alas, do not have courts, and do not keep bands of musicians and do not care about music.

"No doubt there will be violins made and sold in plenty in the future. But they will be quickly made and have a poor tone. For my father's violins, until something remarkable happens in the world of music and musicians can afford to pay as great sums for instruments as dukes and kings used to, there is no future at all."

"No musician will ever be able to pay as much for an instrument as a king or a duke," I said.

"One cannot tell," said Omobono. "One cannot tell."

As for my old master, his violins had never been in demand among the nobility of the land. Now with French, English, Dutch, and Tyrolese makers turning out instruments, the competition was already too much for him. He had sold only twelve instruments since I left him three years before. Of those, though he did not know this, I had bought three myself.

Signora Cattarina could not understand why he did not turn to making something else. Several times she mentioned that carpenters and cabinetmakers were able to support themselves handsomely making and repairing furniture. She could not understand why he did not turn to these things. She thought it only stubbornness that he stuck to the art of the instrument maker, and indeed I myself ventured to ask him why he did not turn to making furniture, continuing to produce violins in his spare time if he wished.

"You ask, too, Thomas?" he exclaimed. "Don't you understand that we are forbidden by God to kill ourselves? And if I turn from making violins to making chairs and tables I would be killing myself. It was not I who decided that I must make violins. It was God Himself. And that is one reason I dedicate my instruments to Him."

He seemed very much older than when I had left him. It was not true that he was drinking heavily all the time as the rough old carter had said. Even Signora Cattarina admitted that.

He had, however, become very discouraged and had lately taken to getting up from his work and just wandering off, never telling anyone where he was going, and not returning for hours. He was certainly not an old man—indeed, was not quite forty years of age. He looked old, however, and had some of the habits of the old. He would, for instance, occasionally start talking to himself, and he would mislay his tools and not be able to find them. I will give you an instance of this. He had a gauge by which he could measure the thickness of the back and top plates of his instruments. That is a very necessary tool for a violin-maker. One day he mislaid it and, search as he might, could not find it again. Another man would then have acquired a new one. But Signor Guarneri took one leg of a pair of compasses, cut a scale on it with a file, and measured the thickness of the plates by pushing the compass leg through them and seeing how much was needed to reach the other side.

Often he just felt the thickness of the plate with his fingers. Such a method of measuring thickness was unheard of. Signor Stradivari would never have used it, because the sharp point of the compass leg left a tiny mark on the finish of the violin—more noticeable inside than outside, where it was largely obliterated by the varnish.

"Why don't you buy a new gauge?" I asked. "Indeed, you could make one very easily yourself."

He shrugged. "I would soon lose it," he replied. Signor

Stradivari, in his will, made my old master a present of many of his tools—planes, knives, files, and two gauges. But Signor Guarneri would not use any of these tools and gave them all away. A very strange man, indeed. He loved Stradivari and yet his pride was hurt when he had to accept help from him.

"What I make must be my own," he said. "Nobody else's." Even using Stradivari's tools would make his work not entirely his own, in his view.

During the short time I spent with him, he would not let me help him. "Your talent is singing," he said. "Don't waste your time trying to make violins." He did, however, let me sing to him and grew quite lively when I sang some of the songs from our productions. When I described my life at the court to him, his dark eyes glowed with pleasure. This was the life that might have been his but for his brother's departure for Venice and his own duty to his father. I told him how his magnificent violin was valued and could make its voice heard over all the other instruments, including some excellent Stainers possessed by the members of the ducal ensemble.

In short, I did everything I could to encourage him, and I hoped now that Signor Stradivari was dead, he would see his way to establishing his own name in the world. Authoritative and free-singing as were his violins, the fact remains that they were all of them a trifle smaller than those of Signor Stradivari. It occurred to me that if he made a bigger instrument, it might be even more splendid. But when I suggested this to him, he shook his head.

"The size of the violin is perfect now," he said. "We have all tried bigger instruments and broken them up. The shape can be varied a little with benefit. But it is in the curvature of the plates, top and bottom, and tuning these to each other, that the best hope for improvement lies." He pulled open an old drawer under his workbench and took out of it a beautiful violin, wrapped in an old blanket. I had never seen this instrument before. The varnish had a ruby glow and the back was of one piece of maple. The scroll was boldly carved, as usual, and with such majesty it seemed an emperor among scrolls.

"When did you make this?" I cried.

"After you left," he replied. "I needed something to occupy my mind. I missed you. It is not named for any duke or count or king. It is the Thomas Soli violin—Thomas Alone."

He tuned it and played that piece of Corelli's which has become known as "La Folia." What a violin—and how he played! It was almost a new kind of instrument—greater than any other violin. It sang clean and true, with power enough to fill a cathedral.

"For you," he said, giving it to me.

"Oh no, master," I replied. "I would not dare take such an instrument from you. I do not deserve to have it."

"You deserve it more than you know," he said. "I have told you that you will never make a violinmaker, that your gift is in singing. Well, you have one other gift, even rarer. It is the gift of cheering men's hearts. You and the violin are partners in that, Thomas. Both of you take men out of themselves and make them a little better—at least for a while."

So I took this violin back to Milan with me but never played it in the Duke's band, for two reasons. First, it would have drowned out even the magnificent Guarneri now in the possession of the first violinist—which would not be wise. Second, the musicians of the Duke's band were many of them abominably careless. As soon as a rehearsal was over, they jostled each other to get out and drink a cup of wine or get a bite to eat. In this unseemly dash, instruments were often broken. So I kept the magnificent Guarneri at the Grancinos', where it was soon famous, and also took it to play occasionally at the home of my patrons the da Nobrigas.

This was a mistake, for they begged me to sell it to them, and my refusal was not well received and started a coldness between us. After a while, I stopped taking it, because of their urgings. They seemed to think that they had a claim not merely on my singing and my playing but on my instrument and myself. One day Signora da Nobriga, after an evening of music, produced the decorated gamba pin which I had made so many years before for Annette.

"Thomas," she said, "it is possible that my husband and I will be going away for a while. You must take this back. We will miss you, dear boy, but my husband is determined to go to London, where he has some business."

This was a great blow to me. To tell you the truth, I had hoped that the da Nobrigas, being childless, might think fit to adopt me, for young men dream constantly of making their fortunes in some such romantic way. Also, I was attached to them.

"I am going to miss you a great deal," I said. "I don't know how I am going to get by without you. I hope you will soon be coming back."

Signora da Nobriga gave me a wistful smile. "Thomas," she said, "much as you may miss us, there is someone I am sure who misses you more."

"And who is that?" I cried.

"Annette," she said. "The pin is hers."

15

One day Brother Cleophas called on me with a surprising suggestion. He was getting a little stiff now and moved more slowly. To turn his head, he had to turn his whole body from the waist, and his singing voice had almost entirely gone, though he ate large quantities of garlic in the hope of restoring it.

He met me at the Grancino home and, having given his respects to that cheerful clan, asked if he might have a word or two with me in private. He was carrying a large parcel wrapped up in some old cloth and tied with several pieces of string all knotted together. When we were alone, he opened the parcel and took out of it the habit of a Benedictine monk.

"I brought this for you," he said. "Remember when you were leaving the orphanage you said you had had a call from God to join our order? Well, the time has come. Put that on."

"Brother Cleophas," I cried, "are you out of your mind? I told you long ago that was all a lie. I made it all up. I have no intention of joining the Benedictines or any other order."

"Lie or no lie," he said, "the fact that the idea occurred to you at all may well have been a vocation, my son. God speaks to us in many subtle ways. And He has sent a distinct sign that you are to become one of us—a sign which is quite plain and can have no other meaning."

"What sign is that?" I asked.

"The one and only bar to your remaining outside of our order has been withdrawn," said Brother Cleophas. "In short—Annette is to be married."

"Married?" I cried, and my heart felt cold as a stone. "To whom?"

"To a fine and honest man in the cloth trade with a place of substance in the world."

"Who is he?" I demanded.

"Signor Antonio Francesca Guilda."

"And who is Signor Antonio Francesca Guilda?"

"He is an honest widower of Milan, in his middle years, with a good business and three small children by his first wife. Ah, my son, it is such a happy match. Signor Guilda has been fully acquainted with Annette's record at the orphanage, with her skills in sewing, embroidering, cooking, and singing. He has interviewed her on several occasions and has handsomely agreed that she is entirely satisfactory and he will provide her with a home as his wife. The wedding is to take place in a week."

"The dog!" I cried. "Annette marry a money-pinching

hound of a merchant with a family already? Never. Does she love him?"

Brother Cleophas shrugged. "What does love matter?" he asked innocently. "Love will not keep her warm in her old age, or feed her either."

"How did they meet?"

"He came to the orphanage inquiring for a bride after his wife had been dead a year."

"You mean he just bought her off the shelf, like a bolt of cloth?"

"No doubt she will come to love him later," said Brother Cleophas innocently. "Strange things happen in the world, my son. Given sufficient time, ice will turn to fire and fire to ice. You yourself, you will perhaps remember, were once aflame for her. But now she means no more to you . . ."

"She means everything in the world to me!" I cried, interrupting him. "She means life and more than life to me. Where is she now?"

"Where but at the orphanage?"

"Then I will go and get her," I said, rising and starting for the door, for I was in such a passion I would have flung out after her on the moment.

"Ho-ho," said Brother Cleophas. "This dog barks loud, but perhaps it is only to keep the horse out of the manger. Why do you suddenly discover this passion for Annette the moment you are going to lose her? Are you sure you would still want her if she was not about to be lost to you?"

"Brother Cleophas," I replied, "it is only when the gates

are about to be slammed shut that most of us rush to get into paradise."

"What a preacher you would have made," he said soberly. "You could bring this miserable world back again to God. Are you sure you will not join us?"

"Quite sure," I said. "But I will thank you for the rest of my life for coming to me with this news."

"In that case," said Brother Cleophas, "if you have children, be sure to have them pray for me. There are some things in my life, my son, including what I am doing now, which I think will require the powerful prayers of children to put to rights."

I did not want to involve Brother Cleophas any further in the matter, and I think he was afraid that I might ask him to help me get Annette away from the orphanage. If he did so and the truth was discovered, he would certainly be severely censored by the Abbot and deprived of whatever little privileges his long years of service had gained for him.

So I thanked him again and sent him on his way. Then I confessed the whole matter to the Grancinos, who warned me that if I was thinking of abducting Annette from the orphanage it might very well cost me my position in the court of the Duke.

"You must expect dismissal," said Giovanni, the eldest. "The Duke cannot countenance kidnap by his servants. There will be complaints by the Abbot and by Signor Guilda. I am surprised you never heard of him. He is a man of some importance."

"What about yourselves?" I said. "Will you be involved

in trouble? You have been kinder to me than anyone else I have known."

"Not at all," said Carlo Grancino. "No one is our master, after all. We live by selling our instruments and making repairs. We are not under anybody's orders. We will help you in any way we can."

"Then I may bring Annette here?" I asked.

"We would be insulted if you took her anywhere else," Carlo replied.

So it was arranged, and the following day I set off from Milan to steal Annette from the orphanage. My plan was a simple one. When I arrived in Cremona and had turned the hired horse in at the livery stable, I went out the back way and, finding a secluded spot, quickly slipped on the habit of the Benedictine monks which Brother Cleophas had brought me. Then I made my way boldly to the orphanage and, ringing the bell, announced to the porter that I had come from Milan and had a package to give to one of the young ladies of the convent.

"Which one?" asked the porter.

"Signorina Annette Occuli," I replied.

"Ah, of course. From her intended, no doubt. Well, give it to me, and I will see that she gets it."

"Thank you," I said. "That is very kind of you. Here is the package. Meanwhile, I am returning to Milan in an hour. I will wait in case she has anything to send in return." The package was, of course, that same gamba peg which I had turned into a brooch for Annette many years before.

Off he went, and after what seemed to me a very very long time he returned, bringing Annette with him. Her face fell when she saw a monk waiting for her, but I said to the porter, "My son, I have something to communicate to this young lady of a private nature. Leave us, then, for a moment."

Off he went, a trifle reluctantly, and I immediately threw back my cowl and Annette gave a little cry and stood staring at me.

"We have only a moment," I said. "Come, put on this habit." And I took off the Benedictine robe and gave it to her. It was woefully big for her, but she pulled it up under the cord around the waist, and it did not look too bad. Benedictines, in any case, do not wear tailored robes. When she had it on, I opened the door, glanced carefully around, and signalled her to follow me.

We had only one bad moment. Just as we were about to leave the great iron gates of the orphanage, a monk approached us from behind, coming up very fast. I was about to run, when he called out, "Thomas, Thomas, are you going to leave me without a word?" Surely enough, it was Brother Cleophas. He had a bundle in his hands, which he gave to Annette. "No bride should be without a dowry," he said. "God bless you both. Remember to have your children pray for me. The prayers of children can take heaven by storm."

We hurried to Cremona, where I found my old friend the carter just about to leave with a cargo of mixed goods for Milan.

"One moment!" I cried. "If you will take us, I will give you four ducats."

He leaned forward and spat carefully between the horse and the shaft and then eyed Annette. "Are the Benedictines so hard put that they are taking in women now?" he asked. "Get her up in the cart and put her under the rug there. Five ducats."

"Agreed," I said, for this was no time to argue. I climbed up beside him, and he shook the reins, and the horse lumbered off. We were not clear of the city before we were overtaken by a group of horsemen who made the old carter stop.

"Have you seen a young woman with white skin, dark hair, and dark eyes, and carrying a bundle of clothes?" they asked.

"I have," said the carter.

"Where is she?"

He turned around and pointed with his miserable whip in the direction of the Church of St. Dominic.

"Over there," he said. "I married her thirty years ago and she's been buried there these past ten years."

"The devil take you for a half-witted fool," said the leader of the horsemen, and they flung down the road to Milan ahead of us.

"I suppose," said the carter when we were on our way again, "you are running away to get married."

"Yes," I replied.

"Is she rich?" jerking his head to the cart where Annette lay.

"No," I replied. "She's an orphan and hasn't a penny in the world."

"What a fool you are," he said. "A young fellow like you, with a passable voice—though it wouldn't do among soldiers, I can assure you—could get himself a plump rich widow without any trouble at all. So why marry her? Her looks won't last."

"Why did you marry your wife?" I asked in reply. He gave me a sharp look, shook his reins at the horse impatiently, and said nothing for a while, merely grumbling to himself.

"There's three fools in this cart," he said at last. "You and me and the horse. And, of the three of us, the horse has the most sense."

16

We were married the next day by a priest of the Dominican order who had known the Grancino family for many years. Assured by them that there was no blood relationship between Annette and me, that we had not been married before, and that both of us were orphans, he performed the ceremony without further questioning.

There was no time to buy a wedding gown for Annette. She was married in a gown borrowed from Signora Francesca Grancino, which with a little adroit pinning and stitching was made to fit her. The generous Grancinos urged us to stay with them until whatever trouble lay ahead had been faced, and indeed I do not know what we would have done without the help of that wonderful family.

The trouble came soon enough. One day after we were married, I reported back to M. Verville.

"Tonnerre!" he cried when he saw me. "You are not in jail? The whole city is looking for you. What a rascal you are—stealing pretty girls from orphanages. What have you done with her?"

"Signor," I said, "I have loved the young lady since we were children. We were brought up in the orphanage together and she is now my wife."

"Charming," he said. "Charming. But also, if you will forgive me saying so—a disappointment. When I was a young man, I managed to elope with several young ladies —one the daughter of a count—and I managed to avoid marrying all of them. Still, after all, you are not French."

He sighed. "A fine tenor," he said. "When they put you in jail, be careful to keep your throat warm. Also, give a little money to the jailer for dry straw to sleep on. That is very important."

"Signor," I said, "you sound as though you have been in jail yourself."

His old eyes sparkled for a moment. "I was not always a withered-up old singing master, ma foi," he said. "No. Once even I was young . . ."

I was in jail in an hour—in fact, in the dungeon of the Duke's castle. This was a huge central underground chamber, only vaguely lit by gratings in the ceiling. Around were a number of cells in which prisoners were kept. I was given a cell of my own, but since the doors of the cells were not barred until nightfall, the other prisoners could stroll around and visit with each other as they pleased.

Some, having more money than the others, had fixed up their cells into quite respectable living rooms. They had cupboards and good beds, and even sacred pictures hanging on the walls. By pulling curtains across the bars, they were able to be completely private, and could be visited by their families, who could even live with them if they wished. Everybody, it turned out, believed he had been imprisoned as a result of some misunderstanding, or as the result of the influence of an enemy. One old fellow told me that he was in jail for something that the Duke did with impunity whenever he wished.

"What is that?" I asked.

"Why, nothing more than issuing my own coins," he replied. "Why should I put His Grace to the trouble of making ducats, florins, and pistoles when I can do the same quite handily myself? Using less silver, too." He was an amusing old rascal, of whom our jailer was very fond. When I heard later that he had escaped, I was not surprised.

It is said that all the world loves a lover, and when I confessed my own reasons for being in prison, I became the hero of the dungeon. Everybody was on my side, and all indignant that, instead of being on my honeymoon, I should be in a dungeon. The prisoner who had the nicest cell, fitted out indeed like an apartment, proposed that I take it over from him for a while and bring my bride to stay with me.

But I could not think of my beloved Annette being in such surroundings, and lived in daily hope that I would be released, or at least given an opportunity to plead my case before the Duke.

The Duke, unfortunately, had gout and was in some part of Switzerland taking the waters. He did not return for three weeks and it was another two weeks before I was brought before him. During all those weeks, though Annette could visit me, and the Grancinos too, I knew very little of what was happening in the world outside. I was astonished, when I was brought into the audience chamber of the Duke, to find the place full of spectators. My case, it seemed, had become a famous one—a sort of operatic plot which was to be played out in real life, with triumph or tragedy depending on the Duke's verdict.

The case against me was made to appear very dark. It was brought out that the Benedictines had taken care of me in my childhood when I was an unwanted orphan. They had given me every protection and help and found me a good master in the person of Signor Guarneri, who had taught me the trade of luthier. I had been allowed, by the kind Signor Guarneri, to join the Duke's court, and the Duke in his benevolence had given me the opportunity to develop my talents as a musician and a singer.

In short, wherever I turned, I had received nothing but kindness.

And how had I repaid this kindness? Why, by the behaviour of a barbarian—a savage. Disguised as one of the monks, I had stolen into the very monastery where I had been so kindly raised, and abducted a young girl who was the promised bride of one of the wealthiest and most sober citizens of Milan—Signor Antonio Francesca Guilda. Signor Guilda was then asked to rise, which he did, and bowed handsomely to the Duke and several of the nobility, who were sitting in chairs around him, and acknowledged the applause of the many friends who had accompanied him to the hearing. I had forced this innocent child into matrimony and deprived her, in so doing, of a husband and a protector with whom she could have lived out her days in respect and comfort. My behaviour was ungrateful, atrocious, and utterly inexcusable. It had brought disgrace on the orphanage in which I and Annette had been raised; it had demeaned the monks; it had made the orphanage an unsafe place in which to raise tender girls, unless I was given the heaviest punishment as a warning for other vagabonds. Ten years' imprisonment, it was suggested, might in some degree mollify my crime.

"Well," said the Duke, turning on me. "What do you have to say about this? Did you steal the girl?"

"No, Your Grace," I said boldly. (It must be remembered, after all, that I was the son of a charcoal burner, and though my father had died in my childhood, still the independence and manliness of that trade was not lost in me.)

"You did *not* steal her?" demanded the Duke. "Yet you are married to her, are you not? Explain yourself."

"Your Grace," I replied, "I was, as you well know, brought up by the good monks at the monastery. And they were very careful to instill into me the exact meaning of every sin, particularly the sin of theft, which is a violation of the Seventh Commandment."

"Come on," said the Duke impatiently. "I want no sermon on theology. Get to the point."

"The point, Your Grace, is that you cannot steal that which nobody owns. In other words, stealing is the sin of illegally taking someone else's property. But my bride did not belong to the monks. They merely had her in their care. She did not belong to Signor Guilda, for she was not yet married to him. She belonged to herself. I did not steal her from herself. She willingly came with me. And now that we are married, she is mine and I am hers and Christ Himself has warned that no man may now steal us one from the other."

In the shocked silence that followed that bold statement, I heard from somewhere in the back of the room the words, "What a preacher he would have made! What a loss to our order!" and knew Brother Cleophas was in the audience.

It was a bold defence, but it was not quite good enough The attorney for Signor Guilda tried to knock it down immediately, saying that Annette had assented to her marriage to Signor Guilda and had in this promised to give herself to him. I had persuaded her to break that promise and had done him great damage in the eyes of his neighbours, in his feelings, and in the amount of money he had already laid out for his wedding. Not only should I be put in prison, then, for ten years, but I should also be compelled to pay Signor Guilda several thousand lire to compensate him for his loss, emotional and material.

It was fortunate that the Duke was more soldier than lawyer, or things would have gone very badly for me, I am sure. As it was, he had begun to favour me through my boldness and he inquired of Signor Guilda just how much money he had laid out on his wedding.

"Be careful about the particulars of your bill," he said.

Signor Guilda had all the particulars ready, and it appeared that his preparations for marriage had cost him one thousand two hundred lire.

"One thousand two hundred!" cried the Duke. "I hadn't known that trade was so brisk among the merchants of Milan. That's handsome, without a doubt. I must ask my steward to look into your tax payments, Signor Guilda. It seems that I am not by any means getting my fair share of your profits."

Too late Signor Guilda realized that, in putting such a fantastic price on his wedding preparations, he had laid himself open to heavy taxation by the Duke.

"Your Grace," he cried, "that is but a paper figure—the actual cost was far less. Far less."

In the end, he agreed that he would be more than repaid if a fine of two hundred lire was levied against me. But that sum was far beyond my ability to pay.

"Come," said the Duke. "Let us see bride and groom here before us. Let them step forward." And so Annette and I, she in a very plain gown and myself in the clothes I had worn in prison, were brought before him. There was a murmur of sympathy from the nobles and gentry seated around.

"What do you say, gentles?" asked the Duke. "Shall we saddle these two young doves with a debt of two hundred lire, and a prison sentence of ten years?"

Nobody wanted to do such a thing.

"Yet there is every evidence that Signor Guilda is out two hundred lire, and nobody comes before my court without obtaining justice," said the Duke.

"My lord," said one of the company, "I find myself monstrously touched by these proceedings. I would be delighted to pay the fine in so good a cause." Several others offered the same, and the Duke turned to me and said, "Well, young fellow, what do you say to this offer of the gentlemen here?"

"I thank them most fully," I replied. "I will be forever in their debt. Yet, since my bride and I are both singers, perhaps we can repay their generosity with a song, if Your Grace permits."

"A song, a song!" everybody cried, and the proceedings became at this point a scene from a play. When all was quiet, Annette, holding tightly to my hand, commenced that lovely aria "When the silvery goddess rises," and we sang it together to tremendous applause, the Duke thumping out the time on the floor as he liked to do.

So, in a kind of farce, but after five weeks in prison, the whole matter ended. We were free to start our lives together. And that all this should have happened forty years ago is a matter of the greatest surprise to me, for it seems but a few days since Annette and I sang our way to freedom and happiness.

17

Though all had now turned out for the very best for Annette and me, it was not so for Signor Guarneri. Despite the death of Signor Stradivari, who had been such an overwhelming competitor for him, he could earn very little from the sale of his instruments. The violin was all the rage. Everybody wanted to play. Teachers thrived, and more and more music, it is true, began to be available for the instrument. But everybody wanted something very cheap.

The Grancinos and the Testores and others, turning out violins very fast, for they had plenty of help, got the greater part of the trade, and could prosper despite the miserable prices paid. French and Dutch violins came into the market in quantities. My old master, with prices down to rock bottom, could not produce instruments fast enough to support himself.

That great instrument he had given to me I produced in the Duke's band occasionally, for my situation there was much more secure than it had been. In short, there was not so much danger of it being resented by the leader of the violins, who, of course, had a Guarneri of his own. Yet, though everybody praised its tone, nobody went to Cremona to seek out Guarneri and ask him for a violin. Most played in the body of the band. There was no need for their individual instruments to be heard above the others, they said. So they were content with instruments that sounded like everyone else's.

"If the day should ever come—it is ridiculous even to think of it—that the violin plays solo like a singer, then Signor Guarneri's instruments may come into their own," one member of the Duke's band said to me. "But it is certainly out of the question to think that at some time people will be content to listen to an hour or more of solo violin playing. If that should happen," he added slyly, "violinists might earn as much as singers." He was jealous that my salary had recently been raised since I now sang all the leading tenor parts both in the Duke's court and at the cathedral.

It was, in a way, bad for Signor Guarneri that his wife now made most of the money needed to live on, out of the silk business. He thought of himself, as a result, as more and more useless and alone. He had, indeed, moments of great bitterness. Once, when I was saying how beautifully a violin of his sounded, he said, "Don't praise me. Thank the silkworms. After all, without them, I could not have bought the wood to make it." Yet there would be times when he was gay and he would ask Annette to sing, for he always loved music.

"You owe me a great deal," he said to me once. "If I had not gone to jail, you would be a bad violinmaker instead of a good singer." That remark provoked him into a strange question.

"Thomas," he said solemly, "is there, do you think, some hidden sense and design to everything that happens in the world?"

It was Annette who replied. "Signor Guarneri," she said, "everything must be part of a magnificent design. Nothing is foolish. It is only because we are so close to it that we cannot see the pattern."

"John the half-wit; my father's wasted life—he is dead now. And my own. All that, really part of a pattern? Surely it is only part of a vast waste of lives, repeated endlessly all over the world in every generation."

"Would you say that the shavings of wood you cut away to make a violin are wasted?" asked Annette. "Haven't they played their essential part? If they were conscious of their part, wouldn't they rejoice to have helped to bring so beautiful a thing into existence?"

He said nothing for a while, and then, turning to me, said, "Your wife not only looks like an angel; she speaks like one too."

My old master became more and more fond of Annette and she of him. She was the only one who could get him out of his black moods and she felt some kind of responsibility toward him, so that at times she would absent herself from me for several days, at the request of Signora Cattarina, to help her husband through a bad time. Much as I missed her, I had not the heart to grumble at these visits. Do we not, after all, owe ourselves to each other? Do we not owe more than we can pay to such men as Signor Guarneri? Who is to replace them when they are gone? They cannot be produced to order.

In the end, something happened that nobody had expected. For all his bouts of drinking (far less in his last years) and his black moods, Signor Guarneri was a strong man with great vitality. That vitality suddenly gave way. He suffered a stroke which paralyzed his left side. The doctors could do nothing for him. He was plunged into the blackest despair. Then his strange character revolted against his affliction.

He had been confined to bed, but he insisted on getting up and dragging himself down to his workshop. There, with the half-wit John watching him, he started to work on one more violin. He could use only his right hand, and yet the very effort of making that instrument (or the vigour of his rebellion against being paralyzed) restored some movement to his left side. In a while he could move his left leg a little, and put some weight on it. Two months later he had back the partial use of the fingers of his left hand, and in a year the violin was finished. But the paralysis showed, for the left side of his face was pulled down and frozen in that position, and he had only partial use of his left hand and arm.

That violin was terrible to look at. The scroll was pitiful; the f-holes were rough and seemed oversize, one lower than the other. I had to try the violin for him, for he could not play himself. I was in terror lest it sound as bad as it looked. But the tone amazed me. There was a glorious bronze sound in the G string, and a high piping loveliness on the E.

"It is a miracle!" I cried. "It is beyond all explanation."

He was very pleased. "Someday maybe they will realize that the tone is all that matters," he said. "The soul, not the body."

My old master died two years later. He was only forty-six years of age at the time. He had no lingering illness, but fell victim to another stroke and died a day or two later, after receiving the last sacraments of the Church.

I helped to clean up his workshop after his death and there on the bench was another violin, the last he made. It was just ready to close, and he must have just pasted in his label before he was struck down. It was the label he always used:

> JOSEPH GUARNERIUS FECIT
> CREMONE ANNO 17— I.H.S.

Maybe, as my wife Annette assured him, there is some great design, by which such lives as his, full of frustrations and a strange loneliness, are fulfilled. I hope and pray that this is so. The contents of his workshop sold for a few lire, and I paid for his last violin myself, for I could find no purchaser for it.

If this were a romance or a fairy tale, I would be able to conclude by saying that my master's violins finally found acceptance, but though I write many years after his death, this is not so. They are still rejected and unknown. Perhaps someday, as that musician said years ago, the time will come when violinists will be in demand as soloists, and then some great violinist will discover my master's instruments and open the ears of the world to them. This is but dreaming, you say? Well, we who were brought up in orphanages know that people must dream, and that sometimes dreams come true. I hope this dream comes true for my old master . . .

Epilogue

Almost a hundred years after the death of Guarneri del Gesù (the name by which he became known to later generations) the dream did come true. During that time his violins, even the many he had made with some care, were neglected. Played in taverns, at fairs; carried about wrapped in cloths or perhaps with no covering at all—it is impossible to say how many were destroyed.

A few discriminating players in their time did recognize the "something extra" in the tone of the Guarneri instruments. Violin solos came into favour, enhancing further the reputation of Stradivari, Amati, and Stainer. But it took a master violinist of as wayward a nature as Guarneri himself to demonstrate the magnificence of his instruments to the world.

That man was Nicolò Paganini, born in Genoa thirty-seven years after Guarneri del Gesù died. Paganini's technique on the violin, his ability to perform the impossible on the instrument, astounded the world, raising the violin to a level far above that achieved by any other instrument. He played so well that the rumour went about that he had sold his soul to the devil in return for his technique. It is ironic that a man supposed to have made a bargain with Satan should achieve his greatest triumphs on a violin made by a man who dedicated every instrument to God.

Paganini was very fond of gambling. As a boy in his teens, touring from city to city, he one day gambled away his violin. He had a concert to play that evening and searched about desperately for any kind of instrument on which to play. A wealthy French merchant, M. Livron, heard of his predicament and offered Paganini a Guarneri del Gesù to play on. Paganini played his concert on the borrowed and comparatively unknown violin. The tone which poured forth from it, revealing every shade of the brilliant technique of the great violinist, created a sensation. "What is he playing on? What is he playing on?" people demanded, and when they were told it was a violin by a maker called Guiseppe Guarneri, nicknamed "del Gesù," they confessed they had never heard of him. Immediately after the concert, Paganini returned the violin to M. Livron, but the generous Frenchman refused it with tears. "I would not dare to play on it," he said. "It is yours and was made for you."

Overnight, the fame that was so long denied Guarneri del Gesù was at last accorded him. Chests, cupboards, attics, shops, storerooms, and taverns were ransacked for his violins. The prices soared and they have never since declined.

Paganini himself preferred his Guarneri del Gesù, the one he had astounded the world with on that day, to every instrument he had, including one by Stradivari. He called it his "cannon," because of the volume of tone it could produce without cracking. He played on it for forty years. When he died, he willed it to Genoa, the city of his birth, where it is now preserved in a special room under a dome of glass. New, it was probably sold for the equivalent of a few pounds. Today, with the possible exception of Stradivari's magnificent "Messiah," it is the most valuable violin in the world and is insured for more than one hundred and twenty-five thousand pounds—though money could never replace it.

There are now possibly fewer than a hundred and seventy genuine violins by Guarneri del Gesù left in the world. Even his worst instruments command the highest prices. The long and cruel neglect of his work is over, and the bitter and lonely man who consoled himself by dedicating his instruments to God is now hailed as a master by every nation on earth.